# 30-minute therapy for

# ANXIETY

everything you need to know
in the least amount of time

Matthew McKay, PhD
Troy DuFrene

New Harbinger Publications, Inc.

## Publisher's Note

*This publication is designed to provide accurate and authoritative information in regard to the subject matter covered. It is sold with the understanding that the publisher is not engaged in rendering psychological, financial, legal, or other professional services. If expert assistance or counseling is needed, the services of a competent professional should be sought.*

Distributed in Canada by Raincoast Books

Copyright © 2011 by Matthew McKay and Troy DuFrene
New Harbinger Publications, Inc.
5674 Shattuck Avenue
Oakland, CA 94609
www.newharbinger.com

Cover design by Amy Shoup
Text design by Michele Waters-Kermes
Acquired by Jess O'Brien
Edited by Elisabeth Beller

---

Library of Congress Cataloging-in-Publication Data

McKay, Matthew.
  Thirty-minute therapy for anxiety : everything you need to know in the least amount of time / Matthew McKay and Troy DuFrene.
     p. cm.
  ISBN 978-1-57224-981-3 (pbk.) -- ISBN 978-1-57224-982-0 (pdf e-book)
  1. Anxiety--Treatment--Popular works. I. DuFrene, Troy, 1972- II. Title.
  RC531.M364 2011
  616.85'22--dc23

                                          2011027692

13      12      11

10   9   8   7   6   5   4   3   2   1                    First printing

# Contents

# Contents

# Introduction

Are you ready to do something about your problems with anxiety? *Thirty-Minute Therapy for Anxiety* is a great place to start. In the sections that follow, you'll find useful ideas and skills you can practice, all of which have helped people live better lives with anxiety.

We wrote *Thirty-Minute Therapy for Anxiety* for people like you and like us: real people with real problems who need a little know-how and a little help—fast. We've made the information in your hands as accessible as we could. Our goal is to give you the information you need in as little as thirty minutes—information about skills and approaches that, with a little practice, can create real and positive results in your life.

Can you really get results in just thirty minutes? That depends on what you mean by "results." If your goal is to get rid of anxiety completely, to make your nervous or worried feelings go away, then no, you can't get those kinds of results in thirty minutes. (In fact, it's likely that you can *never* get those results, no matter how much time you spend. But we'll have more to say about that later.) And if your goal is to have an experience like working with a qualified and experienced mental health expert, you won't find that in these pages. The education and experience it takes to become a therapist is considerable, and no matter how detailed a book may be, nothing you can read is a substitute for working with a qualified professional.

But if you're looking to learn more about your experience of anxiety, then you can make a lot of progress by spending thirty minutes—or even less—with the sections that follow. If you want to learn some simple, evidence-based things you can do to reduce the impact anxiety has on your life, you can certainly get that result from the material in front of you. Are you ready?

# Part 1

# Getting
# Oriented

We've divided the book into four basic parts. In part 1, we'll answer some basic questions you might have about anxiety as a phenomenon. In part 2, we'll introduce you to powerful concepts from *cognitive behavioral therapy*, an evidence-based approach to psychotherapy that has proven effective as a treatment for anxiety and related problems. In part 3, we'll discuss ideas from some other models of psychotherapy. In part 4, we'll cover basic wellness concepts that play into anxiety, such as how to take good care of yourself by eating well, getting active, and taking the edge off anxiety by getting enough sleep.

As you'll quickly see, the parts of the book are divided into short, bite-size sections. In the first segment of each section, we quickly summarize the main concepts and, if we can, give you a little something you can do in that moment so that you can experience what we're talking about. This is kind of like what you might hear during your initial visit to a therapist, so we call these segments What You Need to Know.

As you read along, you may find that the material in a particular What You Need to Know segment doesn't interest you all that much. This is totally fine. Anxiety is a very broad topic, and not all people experience anxiety in the same way. If you find that a What You Need to Know segment isn't for you, let your fingers do the walking and flip ahead to the next section to see where it leads you.

If something in a What You Need to Know segment resonates with you and you want to learn more, you can move on to that section's Taking It Further segment. In therapy, you might have to wait until the following week to go deeper into a topic. Here, just keep reading. In the Taking It Further segments, we expand on what you read in What You Need to Know in a way that can really start to open up your understanding of the topic. These segments include deeper explanations of the section's concept as well as some additional skill- or concept-building exercises.

If you work with a therapist, you might leave each session with small assignments to do before the next session. These could be observations to write down or things to work out on paper, to read, and to do. We've tried to give you the flavor of these useful, between-session activities not only in the exercises provided here, but also in the Practice and Examples segments of this material. Practice and Examples segments are not included in your paper or electronic copy of this book. Instead, you can download the material to your computer or mobile device by visiting **http://9813 .nhpubs.com**.

There you'll find a PDF file that includes exercises, worksheets, assessments, and additional reading, all formatted so that you can easily print or read them on any device. You can access the Practice and Examples material as many times as you like and store it wherever you choose.

How you use *Thirty-Minute Therapy for Anxiety* is totally up to you. You can read through the book from start to finish, or you can scan the table of contents for the particular sections that interest you. You can read the What You Need to Know segments first for a quick overview of the material. Then you can read more deeply in the Taking It Further material in any of the sections that have special interest or meaning for you. And when you're ready to monitor your progress, get more practice at new skills, or read some examples that illustrate the concepts you've just learned, open up your copy of the Practice and Examples file, and you're on your way.

# 1

# What Is Anxiety?

## What You Need to Know

*Anxiety* is a state of uneasiness—focused on the possibility of failure, danger, or misfortune—that causes you distress. Anxiety grows from two sources:

- Physical tension, including fight-or-flight symptoms that are triggered by stress hormones

- Thoughts focused on danger or catastrophic possibilities in the future

The fight-or-flight symptoms occur as our bodies get ready to either run away or do battle with some perceived threat. These symptoms include faintness or dizziness, rapid breathing, sweating, racing heartbeat, clamminess, and so forth.

Anxiety-inducing thoughts, often called *what-if* thoughts, create images and expectations of pain, loss, and disaster. They tell your body to get ready for something threatening or terrible (that is, they activate the fight-or-flight response). But events themselves don't cause anxiety. Rather, it's your thoughts *about* these events, the ways you interpret them, and your physical reactions to these thoughts that produce an anxious emotional state.

The experience of anxiety can be temporary, or it can last a long time. It does appear to be a very essential human experience, familiar to everyone at least sometimes and to some people much of the time. If you're reading this book, we're assuming that, for you, anxiety is a fairly regular experience and one that is causing problems in your life.

..................................................................................................

**Exercise:** What are you worried about right now? Your bills? Your love life? Your health? Are you afraid of heights or elevators or spiders? What about needles or blood? Does the thought of going to a party or giving a speech leave you with a knot in your stomach? Do you wake up at night thinking about that time you got rear-ended in traffic? Do you sometimes find yourself thinking a lot about germs on doorknobs or whether you remembered to turn *all* the burners off on the stove? Maybe one of these questions struck a chord when you read it. Maybe more than one did. All of them have something to do with a kind of human experience we call *anxiety*.

As a prelude to working through the other sections of this book, take some time to assess the areas of your life where anxiety limits you the most. Since you're reading this now, we're guessing you experience anxiety—probably closer to the all-the-time end of the range—and that anxiety is a problem for you some or much of the time, a big enough problem that you've decided to do something about it. Before reading on, can you start to get a sense of how your thoughts and physical reactions contribute to the vicious circle of anxiety?

..................................................................................................

# Taking It Further

When all's said and done, you're probably better off leaving a discussion of the whats and wherefores of anxiety to psychologists and academics. It's probably a lot more useful to figure out how you can live better with anxiety than it is to "know" what causes the feelings in you. But if you're interested, here is some more information.

The simple truth is that no one knows exactly what causes experiences of anxiety. Certainly some instances of anxiety can be traced to specific causes such as major life changes, imminent dangers (for example, natural disasters or health crises), and some medical conditions or side effects of certain medications. But when an episode or a pattern of anxiety can't be clearly tied to a particular trigger or cause, it's safest to say that it's the result of a complex interaction of thoughts and thinking patterns, physical tension, biological predisposition, stressful events in your life, and the conflicting demands of living that we all face. As you'll see, it's not necessary to understand the causes of your anxiety to start doing things to reduce it and to live a better life with whatever anxiety remains.

Anxiety isn't like an infection or a broken bone. There isn't any single treatment or combination of treatments that can "cure" it and make it go away. You've probably heard of antianxiety medications, but keep in mind that their track record for helping anxious people feel better is spotty—they work for some people some of the time. From what psychologists know at this point, it seems that dealing successfully with the challenge of anxiety may require a combination of behavioral, psychological, and some-times even medical treatments—as well as a strong desire to make changes and a certain degree of personal commitment.

........................................................................................

**Exercise:** Are you ready and open to trying the exercises in this book, even when it gets difficult? Where do you fall on the scale of personal commitment to change?

........................................................................................

# 2   What Does Anxiety Look Like?

## What You Need to Know

Even though we speak about anxiety or feeling anxious in a general way, psychologists group a pretty diverse range of behaviors under the broad heading of anxiety. Worry, fear, panic, shyness, the reexperiencing of traumatic events, obsessions, and compulsive behaviors can all be thought of as anxiety-related experiences.

Health care professionals can use clusters of behaviors to diagnose mental health problems, according to criteria set down in *The Diagnostic and Statistical Manual of Mental Disorders*, or DSM (American Psychiatric Association 2000). Even though the DSM is very thorough about describing the criteria for a variety of mental health problems, there is still some disagreement among professionals about differences, if any, between the various anxiety-related disorders. And some psychologists wonder if there isn't more to the phenomenon of anxiety than the behaviors that are associated with it.

Nevertheless, when most of us talk about anxiety, we're not talking about any particular form, like the ones mentioned above. Rather, we're talking about something we're all familiar with—the general sense of being ill at ease about uncertainty.

**Exercise:** Does it matter what label you put on your experience of anxiety? Probably not. Sure, researchers and scholars need a precise, technical language to engage in the science of psychology, and clinicians use this technical language to give structure to the treatments they set up for their clients. But for practical purposes, it doesn't matter whether we have only five of the six diagnostic criteria necessary to *really* have an anxiety disorder. For those of us who are troubled by uncertainty and are ill at ease in our lives, it is enough to know that these experiences of anxiety throw up obstacles between us and what we want our lives to be. If you have even a general sense of how anxiety limits you, you'll be well prepared to choose the exercises in this book that will move you along the path toward living the life you want. Before reading on, think briefly about the role anxiety has played in your life thus far.

# Taking It Further

Because worry and fear are such common features of anxiety, we'll go into a little detail about those here. (If you'd like more detail about the various diagnoses involving anxiety, such as generalized anxiety disorder, panic, and OCD, go to the online segment of this chapter for more information.)

Almost everyone worries, right? And why shouldn't we? Worry can be described as an ongoing attempt to answer the countless significant questions of living: *What if I made the wrong choice? What if I hurt someone? What if I'm not good enough to be loved? What if I can't pay the bills?* Deep down, worry is a fear of uncertainty, the sense that anything, particularly something painful, might happen. Here's one significant point: worry is invariably focused on the future. Worry can't really persist when you're focused on the present moment, on what's happening here and now (which is one of the reasons we discuss practicing mindfulness in section 15). Worry tends to mute much of the richness and pleasure that we might otherwise experience, diminishing what makes us feel vital and alive.

Whereas worry is more general, fear is keenly trained on something specific in the world. You might be afraid of sharks, plane crashes, or blood and needles. You might be afraid of something perilous, such as heights or fire, or something that most people consider harmless, such as balloons or house cats. Unlike worry, which is likely to make you uncomfortable and to sap your vitality if it goes on for long, you can suffer from a significant, persistent fear that doesn't really cause you too much trouble in life. For example, you might be terrified of sharks, but as long as you remain far away from the beach, aquariums, and the nature channels on TV, you can probably organize your life in such a way as to minimize your fear. The problems start, though, when your fears crash into your life and start limiting the things you feel you're able to do: if your dream is to be a lifeguard in Key West, that fear of sharks is going to be a big deal for you.

......................................................................................................

**Exercise:** Is your anxiety experience more about worry or fear, or are you equally troubled by both?

......................................................................................................

More in **Practice and Examples** at http://9813.nhpubs.com.

# 3

## What Does Anxiety Do for Us?

## What You Need to Know

If you struggle with anxiety, you probably spend a lot of time either worrying about having it or trying to figure out how to get rid of it. This is understandable, but it might help to think a little about why all of us get anxious from time to time. The phenomenon of anxiety is actually connected to some basic—and positive—human instincts that sometimes don't work quite right in the world we find ourselves in.

If the fossil record is anything to go by, humans have been roaming the planet for about 195,000 years. And for about 99.7 percent of that time, we had to worry constantly about being eaten or starving to death. Our ancient ancestors worked hard to identify that noise coming from right outside the cave, and they worked equally hard to be certain of having their next meal. They had to. The Middle Stone Age was not a friendly time to be alive, and we have a special name for those of our ancestors who were go-with-the-flow types and not preoccupied with certainty: "extinct."

Even when the threat to our ancestors didn't involve death, it was often something very painful, or at least disagreeable, so our species developed a strong aversion to ambiguity, an aversion that remains very common today despite the fact that the threats most of us face are far from lethal. Anticipating pain is quite enough to trigger these ancient habits, and the desire to avoid this anticipated pain is certainly a big part of our being ill at ease with uncertainty. When most of us are confronted with uncertainty, we try to neutralize it (see sections 13 and 14, on problem solving). Failing that, we keep trying to think up a way to neutralize it, wondering again and again what might happen if... And there you have it: anxiety.

**Exercise:** Look for an example from the past few days where your natural, evolutionarily normal aversion to ambiguity led you into an anxiety spiral. The next time you're faced with ambiguity (don't worry, it will happen soon!), think about the evolutionary value of the mind's reaction to uncertainty and see if this knowledge doesn't change your experience of it, even a little bit.

## Taking It Further

Anxiety engages our natural human drive to solve problems. We don't have sharp teeth and claws. We're not very big compared to other creatures that would like to eat us. But we do have great big brains and the ability to reason and communicate. If your distant, Stone Age ancestors wanted to be certain about something, they thought about it long and hard. And once they had done so, they used their huge brains to figure out what they needed to do to solve their most pressing problems—being eaten or starving to death. This strategy proved so successful that, today, there are nearly seven billion of us, and literally no other organism can compete with us for the top spot on the food chain.

But that evolutionary advantage didn't come without a cost. At some point, our problem-solving prowess managed to protect us from things with teeth and claws virtually all the time. Especially in affluent countries, we figured out how to keep as much food as we could possibly want (and even much more than that) around at all times. Having done this, the smart thing would have been to stop worrying all the time and get comfortable with whatever was going to happen next—but, of course, that's not what happened. Countless generations of ancestors preoccupied with day-to-day survival have inclined us to be a species of worriers and fretters. We *hate* not knowing what's going to happen next, and we instinctively try to solve every problem we imagine we face—even when we know that, really, very many of our problems have no real solutions. You can outwit a lion or a wolf, but what about a feeling of unworthiness or a reoccurring thought that the house might burn down?

..............................................................................

**Exercise:** Imagine a life in which you don't go around trying to be certain about things you can't generally be certain about and trying to solve problems that for the most part can't be solved or aren't problems in the first place. Can you envision letting your big brain take a rest? What would it look like to let some of your problems go "unsolved" *on purpose*?

..............................................................................

# Part 2

# Cognitive Behavioral Therapy

The information in this part acts directly on anxious feelings using techniques from a tradition of psychotherapy called cognitive behavioral therapy, or CBT. Generally speaking, CBT includes techniques that work to identify and change certain thoughts that are irrational, distorted, or otherwise not doing you any good. At the same time, the therapy works to change your behavior—whatever you do that is stopping you from feeling your best.

CBT is the product of several decades of research work. It's not the cure for everything that ails you, but there is a lot of hard evidence that it can and does work for many people. In this part of the book, you'll learn how to relax deeply, cope with worry and panic, face your fears, and solve your problems more effectively.

# 4 Relaxation

## What You Need to Know

You may think you know how to relax, but the type of relaxation that we're about to describe here is a pretty specific technique. To imagine how relaxation training can help you when you're anxious, it helps to first think about how your body feels when you're anxious. Do you tighten your shoulders and hunch them up toward your ears? Knit your brows together? Maybe you clench your fists or go a bit rigid all over. You may even feel sick to your stomach. The relaxation skills we'll teach you in this section will cause real, positive changes in your body. This highly desirable state of deep relaxation was described by cardiologist and mind/body researcher Herbert Benson in his groundbreaking book *The Relaxation Response* (1975). As you enter a state of deep relaxation, your heart rate and respiration will slow down, your blood pressure will drop, and your tight muscles will let go and release tension. Alpha brain waves will increase, resulting in feelings of peace, safety, and serenity. Your anxious feelings will start to diminish as the physiological changes take over.

There's only one trick to this: you'll have to learn and practice at least one relaxation technique until you get the hang of it. The good news is that the techniques are easy to learn, and once you've mastered them, you can do them anytime you need them.

You may settle on one technique that works best for you, or you may prefer to use different ones at different times.

...........................................................................................

**Exercise:** The most basic relaxation technique, and a good one to try first, is deep breathing. Read though these simple steps and then give it a try:

1. Choose a quiet place where you won't be interrupted. Sit or lie down and close your eyes gently.

2. Rest one hand lightly on your stomach and the other just above your sternum. Inhale slowly and gently, drawing the breath as deep into your abdomen as possible. The hand on your chest should remain relatively still, and the one on your stomach should rise a bit.

3. Don't worry about how fast or slow you are breathing; just let the breaths come and go in a way that feels natural and unforced.

4. Once you've settled into a natural rhythm, count each exhalation. When you get to ten, start over again at one. Continue to count your breaths for at least ten minutes, or until you feel relaxed and at ease in your body and mind.

...........................................................................................

## Taking It Further

Once you've tried the deep breathing exercise, you can take things a step further and try a slightly more involved technique, such as progressive muscle relaxation or visualization. These techniques take a bit more practice than deep breathing, but they're still very easy to learn.

Progressive muscle relaxation, or PMR, was developed by Dr. Edmund Jacobson in 1929. PMR involves tensing and relaxing all the muscle groups of your body in a specific order. Practiced daily for several months, PMR can dramatically reduce anxiety and other painful emotions. When PMR was created, it involved a very complex routine, but researchers have since discovered that a much simpler set of exercises works just as well.

..............................................................................................

**Exercise:** Full instructions for PMR are in the Practice and Examples segment, but here's a short version you can try right now:

1. Muscleman pose (tightening arms and shoulders) for 7 seconds. Relax. Repeat.

2. Face like a walnut (hunch shoulders, frown, squint, tighten jaw) for 7 seconds. Relax. Repeat.

3. Back like a bow (arch back slightly while stretching chest and tightening abdomen) for 7 seconds. Relax. Repeat.

4. One or two deep breaths.

5. Toes like a ballerina (tighten buttocks and legs while pointing toes) for 7 seconds. Relax. Repeat.

6. Toes to head (tighten buttocks and legs while pulling toes toward head) for 7 seconds. Relax. Repeat.

..............................................................................................

To use visualization for anxiety, you'll create a peaceful scene in your mind—one you can return to anytime you are anxious. Before you begin to create your peaceful scene, you'll want to get into a relaxed state. Sit or lie down and get comfortable. Use deep breathing or PMR to get into a relaxed state, and then follow the instructions below.

**Exercise:** There are two ways to create your peaceful scene. You can choose an environment that you find relaxing (such as the beach, the mountains, or your childhood home) or you can begin by opening your mind and asking your unconscious to show you a peaceful scene. Either way, close your eyes gently and let a picture begin to take shape in your mind. As the image begins to form, take note of each element of the scene, however small. What do you see? Let the textures and colors take on as much detail as possible. Parts may be bright and clear, and others may be vague and form-less. That's okay. Let your mind and body sink into the moment. Imagine the scents, sounds, and tactile sensations of this relaxing environment. How does your body feel in this place? Are you feeling warm and relaxed? Cool and weightless? You can stay in this peaceful place for as long as you like, and you can return to it anytime to soak in the feelings of serenity and safety. When you feel utterly relaxed and ready to leave your peaceful place, open your eyes slowly and rest for a few more moments.

More in **Practice and Examples** at http://9813.nhpubs.com.

# 5

# Worry Risk Assessment

## What You Need to Know

No matter how hard we try to prevent it, the simple fact is that, sometimes, bad things happen to us. We lose things, we get caught flat-footed, we get sick, and we die. Trying to anticipate where things might go wrong is something that the human mind, with its facility for problem solving, is especially good at. But sometimes the impulse to anticipate and neutralize bad things in our lives can become a preoccupation. We worry. And for some of us, worry can become a 24/7 activity.

........................................................................

**Exercise:** Is worry a serious problem for you? If you can answer yes to any of the following questions, it just might be:

- Are you anxious much or all of the time about bad things that might happen in the future?

- Do you generally expect things to go wrong or get worse?

- Do you tend to worry about events that are very unlikely to occur (a plane crash or shark attack, for example)?

- Do you cycle through the same worries over and over again?

- Are you avoiding doing important things in your life because of your worries?

- Do you find it hard to take constructive steps?

......................................................................

# Taking It Further

People do lose their jobs and get in car collisions—but what are the chances of these things happening to you *today*? Conducting a *risk assessment*, in which you develop a realistic understanding of your risks, can mitigate worry. Your assessment could be as simple as thinking through things in a calm moment. But if this doesn't do the trick, you'll find plenty of food for thought in this section, as well as more detailed instructions for the risk assessment process in the Practice and Examples file.

......................................................................

**Exercise:** While you may read about terrible things happening to a few of us each day, the plain truth is that the majority of people on the majority of days wake up, go about their business, and fall asleep at night without suffering any significant misfortune. If worry is a big part of your life, though, this simple, statistical fact may be lost on you. One way to mitigate worry in your life is to learn how to realistically assess the risks you face in your life each day. As a simple exercise, you can figure out how many times an event happens in a year (plane flights, people riding in elevators, people going out at night, people having stomach pain, and so on), then research how many times the worst happens (plane crash, elevator fall, getting mugged, stomach cancer) and make the calculation to see what your chance is—out of however many millions—of that worry coming true.

...............................................................................

More in **Practice and Examples** at http://9813.nhpubs.com.

# 6 Worry Time

## What You Need to Know

If you've ever tried to talk to other people about your problems with worry, you might have heard some friendly advice: "Well, what can you do? No sense in worrying about it. Just think about something else." Unfortunately, if you're given to worry, it's not likely that anything you do is just going to make it go away. Trying not to think about what you're worried about, in fact, may even make your worrying stronger and more pronounced. But that's not to say there isn't anything you can do to cope with worry.

................................................................

**Exercise:** Instead of worrying all the time and having your worries intrude upon everything you do, set aside half an hour each day during which you worry with focus and intention. When worries come up at other times of day, tell yourself you're going to defer them to that half hour of reserved worry time. If you like, you can note worries on a card or pad of paper so you can remember to worry about them later.

How does it feel to give your worries your complete attention? Does your body react differently than it does when you go about your business and unsuccessfully try to push your worries aside? Are you even able to simply worry for thirty minutes, or do you run out of steam and find the worries dissipating?

................................................................

# Taking It Further

You might have had some interesting experiences when you tried to give your worries center stage for thirty minutes. Sure, your mind is used to worrying, but what happened when you tried to "just worry"? Next time you engage in worry time, try the following exercise to explore the way your past experiences color your worries of the day.

......................................................................................

**Exercise:** During your worry time, consider how your current worries relate to what has actually happened in your life. When you're worrying, do you give historical evidence enough weight in your thinking? Perhaps you think that because you've lived much of your life without catastrophe or calamity, the other shoe has got to drop soon, right? This kind of thinking bears some resemblance to the gambler's fallacy. Imagine that you're tossing a fair coin (that is, not a trick coin, but a garden-variety one that you might find in your pocket). If you toss the coin ten times and each of the ten times it comes up heads, the odds of the eleventh toss being tails are really high, right? Actually, no. The odds of getting tails on toss number eleven are fifty-fifty, just as they were in all the other tosses. If you've lived a relatively calm life to this point, there are likely reasons for it, and chance probably favors more of the same for you. Take this exercise from your worry time to the rest of your day, and try to remember the gambler's fallacy next time you catch yourself waiting for the other shoe to drop.

Perhaps, though, you have the opposite problem: you might be giving too much weight to past events. If something bad has happened to you, you may worry that it might happen again. And, of course, it might. But each event in your life depends on a complex

set of contextual factors that can be at least partially observed and understood. Don't make the mistake of assuming that because you've experienced misfortune once, you'll necessarily experience it again.
......................................................................................................

More in **Practice and Examples** at http://9813.nhpubs.com.

# 7

# Worry Exposure

## What You Need to Know

Even if your worries came to pass, would the outcome be as catastrophic as you fear? Most people who worry a lot consistently predict unreasonably catastrophic outcomes. This is called *catastrophizing*. For example, imagine that a man who worried about losing his job actually did lose his job. But instead of ending up homeless and poor, he got another job. It paid a little less, but he liked the work more. The catastrophic outcome he predicted did not come to pass.

..................................................................................................

**Exercise:** When you worry, your anxiety makes you forget that people routinely cope with even the most serious disasters. You forget that you and your family and friends will probably find a way to cope with whatever happens. For this exercise, choose one of the worries that comes up most often for you. How specifically would you cope if this thing you worry about actually happened? Could you get help? What steps would you take to solve your problem? Imagine every step you'd take to deal with what had happened, picturing it with as much detail as you can.

..................................................................................................

# Taking It Further

Working through the above exercise may not be enough to help you cope with a repeated worry that is more of an obsession. If you're plagued by obsessional worries, try the following exposure exercise.

.......................................................................................

**Exercise:** Make a five-minute recording about your obsessional worry in which you describe the absolute worst thing that could happen. Imagine a total catastrophe, the very worst possible outcome. Include all the details you can think of, but limit the recording to just five minutes. Then listen to the recording over and over. Each time you finish listening and get ready to restart, rate your anxiety on a scale of 0 to 10, where 10 is the worst anxiety you've ever felt. When your anxiety gets to about half of the highest level recorded during that session, stop. Return to the exercise once or twice daily and repeat until your anxiety starts at no more than 2 and quickly drops to 0.

.......................................................................................

# 8

# Exposure for Uncertainty

## What You Need to Know

What keeps worry going is safety behaviors, such as checking, reassurance seeking, and avoiding. These safety behaviors, while briefly reassuring, trigger the next round of worry because they make you want certainty. You immediately start worrying again to see if you are safe or if some danger remains. The problem is, your mind can *always* find danger. The key to reducing worry is to stop or delay safety behaviors and expose yourself to uncertainty. The more you can feel uncertainty and accept the feeling, the less it will bother you and the less you will try to avoid it with worry and safety behavior.

........................................................................

**Exercise:** What safety behaviors do you use to manage your anxiety and worry? Some of them, such as checking, are probably obvious to you. Others may be harder to pinpoint. You might ask your family members and close friends to help you identify reassurance-seeking behavior in yourself. Avoidance is a very common behavior, and in section 16 of this book, Practice Acceptance, you'll find tools to help you understand how avoidance may play a part in your anxiety.

........................................................................

# Taking It Further

Although you might find your safety behaviors helpful in the moment because they may reduce feelings of uncertainty and anxiety, notice that the improvement lasts only a little while, and then uncertainty and worry start growing again.

......................................................................................

**Exercise:** Because safety behaviors actually serve to perpetuate anxiety by preventing exposure to uncertainty, it's important to stop them or reduce them. You can do this by delaying checking or reassurance-seeking behavior for longer and longer intervals during periods of worry and uncertainty. By stopping, delaying, or reducing safety behaviors, you expose yourself to uncertainty, making it less scary and more tolerable. This will ultimately reduce your worry.

......................................................................................

# 9 Relief from Panic

## What You Need to Know

If you've experienced panic, you know the feeling all too well: the rapid heartbeat, shortness of breath, and dizziness, the feeling that you might faint, that all-consuming terror that you might die or lose control, or feeling spaced-out and detached from reality. For some panic sufferers, the depersonalization and unreality are scariest of all because they can make you think you're going insane.

The first step toward overcoming a tendency to panic is to understand why and how it occurs, and to accept that the symptoms can't hurt you. This is necessary because, unlike most other forms of anxiety, panic doesn't center on dangers and events outside the body. It's all about what's going on inside your body—physical sensations that frighten you and lead you to think you're about to lose control. If you are ready to accept that panic symptoms can't hurt you and you're ready to try something new, then dive right into the exercises below. If you first need more information and reassurance about what's happening in your body during the fight-or-flight reaction, see the Practice and Examples file for more details.

........................................................................

**Exercise:** At the earliest signs of panic, use coping thoughts. Remind yourself that these are harmless fight-or-flight symptoms. Although they're unpleasant, they're absolutely normal. They cannot hurt you. You won't faint, die, have a heart attack, stop breathing, or go crazy. No one does during a panic attack. Remind yourself that even though this is unpleasant, you are safe.

## Taking It Further

If you're prone to panic, it's likely that you are overly aware of physical symptoms that you associate with anxiety. Do you check constantly for that initial surge of a racing heart or pay close attention to whether you're getting enough oxygen? Do you check and recheck for signs of detachment or depersonalization? Perhaps you frequently scan your body for feelings of weakness or dizziness. Although this vigilant attitude is intended to protect you by preparing you for the next panic attack, what actually happens is that the vigilance *causes* your panic, feeding the escalating flow of adrenaline.

**Exercise:** Next time you feel panic symptoms coming on, remember the five-minute rule. It takes only three to five minutes for adrenaline to metabolize and disappear from the bloodstream. If you do some breathing exercises and accept the unpleasant fight-or-flight feeling without trying to stop it and without catastrophizing about it, the panic will end in five minutes or less.

More in **Practice and Examples** at http://9813.nhpubs.com.

# 10

# Breath Control Training

## What You Need to Know

How do you breathe when you feel panic? Most people in a state of panic have a tendency to gasp, then take in a breath and hold on to it. Then they take short, shallow breaths, but they don't empty their lungs. Because they're breathing in regularly, they think they should be getting enough air. The problem is, failing to let all the air out creates a disturbing sensation of fullness and a feeling of not getting enough air. That feeling of not getting enough air is just an illusion—a distressing one that causes you to breathe faster and faster. If the cycle keeps going, you'll tip over into hyperventilation, which escalates the cycle of panic.

...........................................................................................

**Exercise:** This breath control exercise, which we've adapted from Nick Masi's audio recording *Breath of Life* (1993), was designed specifically to help with panic disorder. There are five easy steps to follow:

1. Exhale first. As soon as you feel panicked or nervous, or as soon as you become hypervigilant about physical symptoms like a fast heartbeat, completely empty your lungs. You need to exhale first so you have plenty of room in your lungs to take a deep, whole breath.

2. Next, inhale and exhale through your nose. Breathing through your nose slows your respiration down, preventing hyperventilation.

3. Take deep breaths, way down into your abdomen. Place one hand on your stomach and the other on your chest. If you're doing belly breathing, the hand on your stomach will rise and fall while the one resting on your chest will pretty much stay still. Taking deep abdominal breaths will stretch your diaphragm and relax muscle tension that makes it seem like it's hard for you to breathe.

4. Count while you breathe. Exhale first, and then breathe in through your nose, counting, "One…two…three." Pause a second, then breathe out through your mouth, counting, "One…two…three…four." The counting protects you from rapid, panicky breathing. To ensure that you empty your lungs fully, always make your exhalation one beat longer than your inhalation.

5. Now, slow your breathing down by one beat compared to the pattern in step 4. Breathe in and count, "One…two…three… four," then pause and breathe out, counting, "One…two… three…four…five." As before, be sure to breathe out one beat longer than you breathed in.

........................................................................................

## Taking It Further

Breath control training is very effective, and with practice you can prevent the worst of your fight-or-flight symptoms. However, it's important that you start out by practicing only in a calm and safe environment, not when you are panicky or anxious.

......................................................................................

**Exercise:** Get used to breath control training by practicing at a time and place where you are calm and unlikely to be interrupted. After several weeks of daily practice, the technique will be "over-learned" and you'll be able to easily slip into this mode of breathing in situations that make you slightly nervous. As you get better and better at it, you can try using it at times when you are worried about panic or troubled by physical symptoms.

Before you think about trying breath control training during a full-blown panic, move ahead to the next section and master interoceptive desensitization. In learning that technique, you'll get the practice you need so that you can slow your breathing even during the most disturbing anxiety symptoms.

......................................................................................

More in Practice and Examples at http://9813.nhpubs.com.

# 11 Interoceptive Exposure

## What You Need to Know

Desensitization is one of the most effective techniques used to treat panic disorder, and also one of the most challenging. Most of the following exposure exercises were developed and tested by Michelle Craske and David Barlow (2008), and they are intended to induce feelings similar to those many people report prior to or during a panic

What you're about to do is re-create, in a safe way, bodily sensations similar to those you associate with panic. You'll learn to experience dizziness, rapid heartbeat, and even feelings of unreality as simply annoying effects of your body's normal fight-or-flight reaction. Once you get in the habit of not associating these feelings with panic, you'll find you're no longer overly focused on your bodily sensations.

......................................................................................................

**Exercise:** In the first stage of desensitization, you briefly expose yourself to ten specific sensations and then rate your reactions. As you prepare to do the actions on the list below, you will probably notice that some of the sensations will be quite uncomfortable. But it is precisely the feelings you most fear that you must desensitize to in order to recover from panic disorder. If exposing yourself to these physically arousing experiences feels too frightening to do alone, enlist a support person to be present throughout the exercise. Later you can discontinue support as you get more comfortable with the sensations.

1. Shake your head from side to side for 30 seconds.

2. Lower your head between your legs, then lift it. Repeat motion for 30 seconds.

3. Run in place (check with your doctor first) for 60 seconds.

4. Run in place wearing a heavy jacket for 60 seconds.

5. Hold your breath for 30 seconds or as long as you can.

6. Tense major muscles—particularly in your abdomen—for 60 seconds or as long as you can.

7. Spin while you sit in a swivel chair for 60 seconds (don't try to spin while standing up).

8. Breathe very rapidly for up to 60 seconds.

9. Breathe through a narrow straw for 120 seconds.

10. Stare at yourself in a mirror for 90 seconds.

........................................................................................

# Taking It Further

As you expose yourself to each of the ten sensations, you'll need to keep records to identify which ones create the most anxiety and have the greatest similarity to your panic feelings. When rating your anxiety intensity, the scale ranges from 0 to 100, where

100 is the worst anxiety you've ever felt. When rating each exercise's similarity to panic sensations, the range is from 0 percent similarity to 100 percent, for absolutely identical feelings.

The next stage of desensitization involves making a hierarchy of frightening sensations. On the Interoceptive Assessment Chart that you'll find in the Practice and Examples file, check off each exercise that you rated 40 percent or above in similarity to actual panic sensations. On the Interoceptive Hierarchy/Anxiety Intensity Chart (also provided in the Practice and Examples file), rank the checked exercises from the least to the greatest anxiety-intensity rating.

Once you've developed your hierarchy, it's time to begin the actual desensitization process. Start with the item lowest in anxiety on your hierarchy chart. If you need to have a support person present during initial exposure, that's fine. Here's the actual desensitization sequence:

1. Begin the exercise and note the point where you first experience uncomfortable sensations. Stick with the exercise at least thirty seconds after the onset of uncomfortable sensations—the longer the better.

2. As soon as you stop the exercise, rate your anxiety.

3. Immediately following each exercise, begin controlled breathing.

4. Following each exercise, remind yourself of the harmlessness of the bodily sensations you're experiencing. For example, if you feel light-headed or dizzy after rapid breathing, remind yourself that this is a temporary and harmless sensation

caused by reduced oxygen to the brain. Or if you have a rapid heart rate after running in place, you could remind yourself that a healthy heart can beat two hundred times a minute for weeks without damage, and it's certainly built to handle this little bit of exercise.

5. Continue trials of desensitization with each exercise until your anxiety rating is no more than 25.

More in **Practice and Examples** at http://9813.nhpubs.com.

# 12 Fears and Phobias

## What You Need to Know

Are you plagued by fears or phobias? If so, it's likely that you'll do almost anything to avoid the feared object or situation. This is a normal reaction, but the truth is that the way to get over a fear is to expose yourself directly to the thing that terrifies you. The good news is that you don't need to do it all at once; you can move forward slowly by using a hierarchy that you create yourself, moving through the steps of an exposure hierarchy until you can contact your fears up close and loosen their hold on you for good.

....................................................................................

**Exercise:** You can work on your phobia through real-life exposure to your fear, or by using imagery if you can't create a hierarchy of real life situations. The premise of a hierarchy is that facing your fear in small increments will help you ultimately face the feared object or situation itself. For this exercise, create a hierarchy of six to twenty items in which the first item on your list is the least unpleasant version of your most feared object or situation, and the items that follow are progressively more anxiety-provoking. Take, for example, a fear of dogs. Your first item might be a cartoonish drawing of a friendly looking dog. The next one might be a photograph of a dog, and next could be sitting at a good distance from a thoroughly restrained dog, and so on until you reach what seems to you the scariest dog-related situation—perhaps having a large, exuberant dog run up to you and jump up on you.

There are four main variables to manipulate as you create your hierarchy: how physically close you are to the feared object or situation, how close you are in time to the feared object or situation or how much time you spend exposed to it, how difficult and scary the situation or scene is, and how close you are to a support person.

# Taking It Further

Before you try exposure to the easiest item on your hierarchy, work on relaxing your body for ten minutes. As you've learned elsewhere in this book, relaxation is all-important in dealing with anxiety. We recommend that you use deep breathing before and after your exposure work. You can repeat to yourself phrases such as these:

- *Breathe and relax.*

- *Release and let go.*

- *Breathe away stress.*

You may also wish to use coping thoughts before and after (but not during) exposure. General coping thoughts such as the following can help you relax:

- *These feelings will pass.*

- *I've been through this before, and I'll get through it just fine this time.*

- *My natural fight-or-flight reactions can't hurt me.*

- *If I get an adrenaline rush, it will only last a few minutes provided I don't get into a worry spiral.*

**Exercise:** Once you are in a thoroughly relaxed state, begin by exposing yourself to the first (easiest) item on your hierarchy. Set a timer for 60 seconds, during which you will stay in contact with the object or situation, or immerse yourself in detailed mental imagery if you are doing an imagery hierarchy. When the timer goes off, rate your anxiety on a scale of 0 to 10, where 0 is no anxiety and 10 represents the worst fear you've ever felt. If you get overwhelmed and withdraw from an exposure, relax and immediately reenter the exposure situation. If you find yourself retreating repeatedly, you should divide that step of your hierarchy into smaller, easier steps that you can complete.

Relax and use coping thoughts between scenes or steps. Repeat until your anxiety level goes down. Move on to the next item on your hierarchy when your anxiety declines to a tolerable level, say 2 or 3 on the scale. It usually takes at least two exposures to fully desensitize to a scene. The lowest-ranked scenes, where your anxiety is quite low from the outset, may be exceptions.

Practice daily. Your first practice session should last about twenty minutes. Later you can extend imagery exposure sessions to as much as thirty minutes. The main limiting factor is fatigue. Always stop a session if you begin to feel tired or bored. Expect to master from one to three hierarchy items during each practice session. When starting a new practice session, always go back to the last scene you successfully completed. This helps you consolidate your gains before facing more anxiety-provoking items.

More in **Practice and Examples** at http://9813.nhpubs.com.

# 13

# The Role of Problem Solving

## What You Need to Know

Sometimes, the things you feel anxious about are complex problems in your life. We're not talking about very elusive questions that, in fact, aren't really solvable problems at all. If you worry that you're not a good person or that you're not lovable, you should probably focus your time and attention on your perceptions or thoughts rather than your problem-solving skills. It probably wouldn't do you any good to design a stepwise plan to solve the "problem" of your essential worth as a human being. But for problems that are related to a specific, in-the-world outcome about which you're concerned, skillful problem solving can be a significant asset.

There's a point in what we just said that bears restating: It's very useful to know which of the struggles in your life are problems to be solved and which are just things that you'd be better off to acknowledge, accept, and take as they are (for more on acceptance, see section 16). Telling the difference is among the most important things you can learn as you move forward in your life with anxiety.

..................................................................

**Exercise:** How can you tell which problems can be solved? It may take some practice, but it's not especially hard to identify those experiences that need problem solving and those that don't. To help you decide on a particular issue, write down your responses to the following:

1. I feel anxious about:

2. The worst thing that could happen is:

3. The best thing that could happen is:

4. Could a group of three or more reasonable people agree about the conditions that would need to be met in order for the best thing to have happened?

5. True or false: If the best thing that could happen *did* happen, I would feel much less anxious or upset about this particular issue.

For the first three questions, did you write down something specific and concrete, having to do with the way people or things are in the world? If you did, problem-solving may be right for your situation. If what you wrote was abstract, relating to judgments or feelings, problem solving may not be a good use of your time.

The next question attempts to clarify whether you actually have a problem with a coherent solution or solutions. Three reasonable people might not be able to agree on the best means to a solution, but they probably could agree on what the outcome of the solution should be. If three reasonable people couldn't agree on the best outcome, chances are you're dealing with an issue that, really, is more of a perceptual issue than a problem.

Finally, if you could somehow arrive at the solution, would you feel any better about your situation? Or would solving this problem change very little about your state of mind? If making a single concrete change, even if it is complex and significant, might change your outlook significantly, problem-solving may be a good approach for you. Detailed instructions for effective problem solving can be found in the next section.

# 14     Steps to Problem Solving

## What You Need to Know

Problems that elude solution result in chronic emotional pain. When your usual coping strategies fail, a growing sense of helplessness makes the search for novel solutions more difficult. The possibility of relief seems to recede, the problem begins to appear insoluble, and anxiety or despair can increase to crippling levels.

In 1971, Thomas D'Zurilla and Marvin Goldfried devised a five-step problem-solving strategy for generating novel solutions to any kind of problem. They defined a problem as "failure to find an effective response." For example, the fact that a person can't find one of his shoes in the morning is not in itself a problem. It becomes a problem only if he neglects to look under the bed, where the shoe is most likely to be found. If he looks in the sink, the medicine cabinet, and the garbage disposal, he is beginning to create a problem—his response is not effective in finding the missing shoe, and, therefore, the situation becomes "problematic."

A convenient acronym for the five steps of problem solving is SOLVE, which stands for:

1. **State your problem.** The first step in problem solving is to identify the problem situations in your life, using the checklist in the Practice and Examples segment if necessary.

2. **Outline your goals.** Next you'll examine what you've been doing and how this relates to how you feel and what you want.

3. **List your alternatives.** This is a brainstorming phase that encourages creative approaches to reaching your goals. When you finish this step, you'll have lots of alternative strategies in hand.

4. **View the consequences.** In this step you'll assess the various possible outcomes of different strategies and select which ones to try.

5. **Evaluate your results.** Here's the rewarding part—put the strategies into action and see what happens!

.....................................................................

**Exercise:** Problem solving is effective for reducing anxiety associated with procrastination and the inability to make decisions. It is useful for relieving the feelings of powerlessness or anger associated with chronic problems for which no alternative solution has been found. Can you think of ways in which a lack of problem-solving skills exacerbates your anxiety?

.....................................................................

## Taking It Further

Now you have an overview of the problem-solving process and have given some thought to how a lack of problem-solving skills may be exacerbating your anxiety. If you'd like to work on your problem-solving skills, the rest of this section will guide you through the process, step-by-step.

## Step 1: State Your Problem

The first step in problem solving is to identify the problem situations in your life. You might be experiencing problems with your finances, work, social relationships, family life, and so forth. We've included a checklist in the Practice and Examples segment that will help you choose the area or areas you want to foucs on as you develop your problem-solving skills.

## Step 2: Outline Your Goals

Now, it's time to set one or more goals for change. Examine your response to the problem—what you do, how you feel, and what you want. These statements, in particular, are helpful for developing specific goals.

- What is the situation? (Choose from the Problem Checklist or describe it briefly in your own words.)

- Who else is involved?

- What happens? (What is done or not done that bothers you?)

- Where does it happen?

- When does it happen? (What time of day? How often? How long does it last?)

- How does it happen? (What rules does it seem to follow? What moods are involved?)

- Why does it happen? (What reasons do you or others give for the problem at the time?)

- What do you do? (What is your actual response to the problem situation?)

- How do you feel? (Angry? Depressed? Anxious? Confused?)

- What do you want? (What things do you want to change?)

Based on the problem analysis above, what are your goals?

- _____

- _____

- _____

## Step 3: List Your Alternatives

In this phase of problem solving, you brainstorm to create strategies that will help you achieve your newly formulated goals. The brainstorming technique set forth by author Alex Osborn in 1963 has four basic rules:

1. **Criticism is ruled out.** This means that you write down any new idea or possible solution without judging it as good or bad. Evaluation is deferred to a later decision-making phase.

2.  **A freewheeling approach is welcomed.** The crazier and wilder your idea is, the better. Following this rule can help lift you out of mental ruts. You may suddenly break free of your old, limited view of the problem and see it in an entirely different light.

3.  **Quantity is best.** The more ideas you generate, the better your chances are of having a few good ones. Just write them down, one after another, without thinking a lot about each idea. Don't stop until you have a good, long list.

4.  **Combination and improvement are sought.** Go back over your list to see how some ideas might be combined or improved. Sometimes two pretty good ideas can be joined into an even better idea.

Brainstorming during this phase should be limited to general strategies for achievement of goals. Leave the nuts and bolts of specific actions for later. You need a good overall strategy first. For each of your goals, come up with at least ten alternative strategies and write them down.

## Step 4: View the Consequences

By now you should have several goals, each with a number of strategies for how you will accomplish it. The next step is to select the most promising strategies and examine the consequences of putting them into action. For some people this process of figuring and weighing consequences happens automatically as soon as they think of a possible strategy for getting what they want.

Others are likely to ponder the consequences more slowly. Whichever category better describes you, it will be helpful to do this step thoroughly and conscientiously.

Pick the goal that is most attractive to you. Go over its strategies and cross out any obviously bad ideas. Whenever possible, combine several strategies into one. Try to reduce your list to three strategies representing your best ideas. Now you can use the Evaluating Consequences form in the Practice and Examples segment, or you can make a choice based on a gut feeling of which strategy is best.

## Step 5: Evaluate Your Results

The last step is the hardest, because it's time to act. You've selected some new responses to an old situation. It is time to put your decisions into effect.

Once you have tried the new response, observe the consequences. Are things happening as you predicted? Are you satisfied with the outcome? A sense of satisfaction means that the new response is helping you reach your goals in a way your old attempts were not.

If you are still not reaching your goals, return to your alternative strategies list. You can either generate more ideas at this point or select one or more strategies that you passed over before. You may repeat steps 3, 4, and 5 of the problem-solving procedures.

You might feel a little overwhelmed by the complex steps involved in problem solving. You might be thinking, *Do I really have to do all that?* The answer is yes—the first time. Because you've been stuck for a while in a problematic situation and your old, habitual solutions haven't worked, we recommend that you follow each step of the technique to identify and then achieve your goals. Later you can tailor the procedures to fit your particular style, and much of it will have become automatic.

More in **Practice and Examples** at http://9813.nhpubs.com.

# Part 3

Other Ways to Live Well with Anxiety

If you've made it this far, you're now armed with some well-tested and proven cognitive behavioral tools. In this part of the book, we're going to look at some different approaches to living well with anxiety. In the first five sections, we're going to explore some ideas that come from a newer kind of behavior therapy called *acceptance and commitment therapy*, or ACT for short, which is pronounced like the word and not as separate letters. ACT encompasses a whole body of work in behavior therapy, and it has been successfully applied to a pretty amazing range of psychological and health problems, from anxiety and depression to diabetes and even racism and stigma. Psychologists believe that ACT is so effective at treating such a wide range of "problems with living" because it addresses these issues at a very basic level, targeting several aspects of behavior that, ACT assumes, underlie everything we do, both good and bad. Now that we've told you this, though, you can go ahead and forget that you ever heard about ACT. Each part of the therapy relates to some very simple, very commonsense ideas about living—and that's how we'll be talking about them in the sections to come.

After that, we'll look at some other skills from yet another model of psychotherapy, this time *dialectical behavior therapy*, or DBT. Like ACT, DBT is a newer approach to psychotherapy, one that was developed initially to deal with *borderline personality disorder*, or BPD, a very serious psychological problem that affects some people. DBT was among the first treatments for BPD that proved to be effective. As interest in DBT grew, psychologists started to experiment with applying DBT to other problems. What you'll find in the sections that follow is just a little sliver—a couple of skills from the DBT package that we think might be of use to you for the self-care of anxiety. You'll practice distinguishing primary emotions from secondary ones, examine your anxiety-making behavior patterns, identify and reframe trigger thoughts, make room for positive feelings, and discover tools for distraction and self-soothing.

# 15  Be Mindful

## What You Need to Know

One way to take the teeth out of anxiety is to concentrate more of your attention on what is actually happening to you right now, in the present moment. The deliberate and structured approach to keeping your attention in the present moment is sometimes called *mindfulness*.

As a concept, mindfulness has been around for a long time. It's often associated with Buddhism, which regards right mindfulness as one element of the Eightfold Path out of suffering, but it's not necessarily Buddhist or even religious. Rather, mindfulness is just something you can choose to do in the world. Noted mindfulness authority Jon Kabat-Zinn has famously defined mindfulness as "paying attention in a particular way: on purpose, in the present moment, and nonjudgmentally" (Kabat-Zinn 1994, 4). For our purposes, there's no need to add any more baggage to the idea of mindfulness than this. A key component of mindfulness is mindful breathing, which is easy to learn.

.....................................................................................

**Exercise:** To breathe mindfully, observe your breath from the nose to the diaphragm. Count each exhale until you reach ten and then begin again with one, or simply say "in" and "out" to yourself on each inhalation and exhalation. As you breathe, observe your thoughts without judgment—perhaps labeling each one as "thought"—and then return your attention to the breath.

..............................................................................

# Taking It Further

There are a couple of things you need to know about engaging with mindfulness (and these two are *really* important).

One of the wrinkles about mindfulness practice is this: the idea that you need to do it for no reason at all is essentially built into the whole concept. To do the practice right, you really do need to *just* pay purposeful and nonjudgmental attention to *whatever* is happening. If you engage in mindfulness practice with the goal of feeling less anxious, you're likely to be scanning your body and mind looking for anxiety and waiting for it to show up. According to the principles of the practice, though, you should be simply experiencing whatever is happening at the moment. The harder you look for anxiety, the less mindful of the present moment you'll be. So, if you can, try to come to mindfulness on its own terms. Learn to just sit and see what happens. As you find and deepen your practice, you're very likely to find that anxiety relaxes the grip it has on your life. But, paradoxically, this is only likely to occur if you don't try to make it happen.

Another thing you should know—or that you'll soon find out when you try: mindfulness is a skill that takes time and practice to develop. The overwhelming majority of us have a lifetime of practice at maintaining a busy, grasping, and clinging mind.

Learning to quiet our minds, simply be aware, and gently let go of our thoughts takes effort. It can feel very strained and awkward sometimes, as any meditator is likely to tell you. Patience and perseverance are the keys to success, though, and the path you'll walk as you go is likely to be interesting and instructive. You meet your own mindfulness practice wherever you are and take it from there.

...............................................................................................

**Exercise:** Once you've practiced some mindful breathing and made a commitment to bringing mindfulness into your everyday life, here's another basic exercise you can try. You probably won't want to make a regular practice out of it, but it will help you get into a mindfulness groove.

1.  Find a quiet place in a room where you won't be disturbed for a few minutes, someplace you spend a fair amount of time and with which you're familiar.

2.  Set some kind of timer for ten minutes.

3.  Find a place on the wall that doesn't have anything hanging on it and turn to face it. You can stand, sit in a chair, kneel—whatever is comfortable. Get as close to the wall as you can while still being able to focus clearly with your eyes on the details of the paint, wallpaper, stucco, or whatever else is covering it.

4.  Now take three deep, slow breaths.

5.  Once you complete the third exhalation, let your eyes focus on the wall. Really look at it. What can you notice about the texture? The material itself? Is there heat coming off the wall? Light? Does the wall have a smell? If you feel like it, you can even taste the wall. Use any or all of your five senses to really, really take in the wall.

6. As you go, you're likely to be struck by certain thoughts: "What the hell? I just licked the wall!" This is natural and normal. Your job here isn't to *not* think thoughts. Your job is to just notice and appreciate the wall. If thoughts come up, let them come up. And then let them go as you return to your task of getting to know your wall very, very well.

7. At the end of ten minutes, your timer will ring—probably to your great relief. Before you go back to your day, though, reflect for a moment on your engagement with the wall. Did you notice anything you've never noticed before? Did anything surprise you about your wall? Did you find your breathing slowed down or sped up? What about your pulse? Did you feel hot or cold? If you're struggling with anxiety in your life, did you feel it more or less while you were contemplating the wall? Keep in mind that the goal of the exercise is only to give you a taste of conscious attention to the present moment, not to ease your anxiety. But when you were intentionally and flexibly focused on the wall in the here and now, did you feel the tug of worry and ill ease like you normally do throughout the day?

..............................................................................

Congratulations. If you did this exercise in anything close to the spirit we intended, you just practiced a little bit of mindfulness. Keep exploring this idea and see where it takes you. Using this exercise as inspiration, think about some other quotidian objects and activities that can become part of your budding mindfulness practice. The Practice and Examples section contains a list of ideas for practicing mindfulness in everyday life.

More in **Practice and Examples** at http://9813.nhpubs.com.

# 16  Practice Acceptance

## What You Need to Know

After plowing through the previous sections, are you still worried that bad things might happen to you? Good. Bad things might happen. In fact, bad things will happen, they might be happening right now, they might be things you've never even imagined might give you grief, and there's nothing at all you can do about it.

Whoa! What kind of talk is that for a book on anxiety?! We're not trying to be grim and morbid, but telling you that things might go wrong in your life isn't exactly news. The flip side of this observation isn't news either, but maybe you haven't thought about it much before now: Just because you think something might go wrong doesn't mean that it will. And the mere fact that you think a thing or a situation is a certain way doesn't mean that it is so. These two assertions, that things will go badly from time to time and that everything isn't as you suppose it to be, underlie the discussion of acceptance in this section.

When we talk about acceptance, we mean adopting, on purpose, an open, receptive, and nonjudgmental attitude toward the experiences you have as you live your life—the good and bad, the pleasurable and painful, the bitter and sweet. We're speaking broadly here about all kinds of experiences: your interactions with the world and the people in it, your thoughts and sensations, and your feelings—even your feelings of anxiety. The opposite of acceptance is *avoidance*, for obvious reasons. If you don't accept an experience that comes your way, you will seek not to have it. Avoidance comes in many flavors: running away, refusing to engage, taking a drink, and so forth. If you're struggling with anxiety, pay attention to avoidance. It matters. The things you find yourself avoiding are very likely the things you're anxious about.

...........................................................................................................

**Exercise:** Are there areas of life where you have an easier time with accepting what is? How about areas of life where avoidance rears its head most of the time? Give a bit of thought to your current tendencies before moving on to the next segment.

...........................................................................................................

# Taking It Further

Acceptance, as we mean it, is independent of desire and judgment, and this includes both positive and negative judgments. When you accept a particular experience, you acknowledge it, stay present to it, and take it in without attempting to alter it in any way. You don't have much control over what thoughts come up after that. You might very well react negatively: *I don't like it!* But a negative reaction doesn't equal avoidance, which demands that you act to reduce, eliminate, or control your experiences.

By willingly and openly engaging with what *is*—by cultivating acceptance—you're liberated to imagine and move toward what might be. When you decide that something must not or should not be—*I mustn't be uncomfortable riding in an elevator, I can't allow myself to seem stupid in front of my peers*—you take away some of your options for living. Your world gets just a little bit smaller. Over a lifetime, avoidance of what *is* can confine you to very small places. The cost of persistent avoidance can literally be your life.

We get that acceptance might not sound that great to you right now. Most of us have a tendency to run from discomfort, and in a time when it seems like avoiding suffering is as easy as making a trip to the pharmacy or the liquor cabinet, it can be hard to take that leap into trying acceptance when things get rough. And since we're sold on the idea that you should decide where you want to go in life and then head off in that direction, even if that means feeling some pain along the way, we know we may sound kind of stoic to you here. Keep this in mind, though: we're not talking about grim resignation. Acceptance isn't about giving up; it's about opening up—to possibilities, alternatives, and the fringe benefits that sometimes come with really hard experiences. It's a process that we sincerely hope you're willing to test and try out, at least for a while.

........................................................................................................

**Exercise:** Now that you've considered the issue of acceptance versus avoidance in your life, can you see what avoidance has cost you? On a small card that you can carry with you, list three ways that avoidance has limited you. Review the card at least once a day and let yourself feel how opening up in these areas might give you more options and make your world feel just a bit bigger.

........................................................................................................

More in **Practice and Examples** at http://9813.nhpubs.com.

# 17

# Observe Your Thoughts

## What You Need to Know

Defusion, a component treatment of acceptance and commitment therapy (Hayes, Strosahl, and Wilson 1999), is a technique that changes your relationship to your mind and your thoughts. The term was coined by Steve Hayes and refers to the Buddhist practice of observing and distancing from your mind. Instead of "fusing" with painful cognitions and getting caught in long chains of fearful or depressing thoughts, defusion helps you watch and let go of even the most disturbing mental chatter. This section and the next two will teach you how to defuse from your thoughts.

The practice of observing your mind and then labeling and releasing thoughts helps you detach and take your thoughts less seriously. Instead of *being* a thought ("I am ugly" or "I'm in danger"), defusion teaches you to simply *have* them ("I am *having a thought* that I'm in danger" or "I am *having a thought* that I'm ugly"). *Being* a thought makes it seems absolutely true, and gets you fused and stuck with it. *Having* a thought helps you recognize that it is *just a thought*, one of about sixty thousand you'll have in a day. You can let it pass through and drift away. The starting point for defusion is learning how to watch your mind. A good initial exercise for this is the following meditation.

...........................................................................................

**Exercise:** Imagine that you are in a white room, completely empty of furniture or any adornments. You can position yourself anywhere in the room—at the ceiling, on the floor, or in one of the corners. But wherever you put yourself, visualize an open doorway on your left and a second open doorway to your right. The doors open onto darkness; you can't see anything beyond. Now imagine that your thoughts are entering from the doorway on your left, passing across your field of vision, and exiting through the doorway on your right. As your thoughts cross the room, you can attach them to a visual image (a bird flying, an animal running, a hulking mafioso, a balloon, a cloud, or anything else). Or you can simply say the word "thought" to yourself. Don't analyze or explore your thoughts. Let them each have a brief moment in your awareness and then exit through the doorway to your right.

Some thoughts may feel urgent or compelling, and it may seem that they want to stick around longer than others. Just let them move on out the door to make room for the next thought. As new thoughts show up, make sure you've relinquished the old ones, but don't worry if the old ones show up again. Lots of thoughts tend to repeat themselves, and the visitors to your white room may be no exception.

Do the exercise for five minutes. When you've finished, we'd like you to notice some things about the experience. First, did your thoughts speed up, slow down, or remain at about the same rate? Second, how easy or hard was it to let go of each thought and make room for new ones? Third, did your thoughts feel more urgent and engaging, less engaging, or about the same? Finally, did you feel calmer, more tense, or about the same?

For many people, the mere act of observing thoughts slows them down and makes them feel less urgent. Some people experience greater calmness because they are watching instead of being fully caught up in their thinking.

...........................................................................................

# Taking It Further

There's a very intimate relationship between defusion and contact with the present moment. If you're tearing through life as fast as you can go, with your sights set on something, anything, out in the future, it's very likely that your thoughts of the moment will exercise a lot of control over your actions. Slowing down, even a little, by practicing observing your thoughts, is a good way to start seeing when you're acting automatically on some thought you've had. Has your car ever made a disconcerting noise while you were driving, only to run silent and tight as a drum when you took it to the mechanic? It's hard for a mechanic to fix a noise without hearing it. If the mechanic had the time to sit quietly with your car as it rolled down the road, the sound would eventually start up again, and then the process of fixing the problem would be a whole lot easier. It's kind of like that with your thoughts—except that you can easily make the time to sit and pay attention to your thoughts. The next exercise will help you learn how to do that.

.............................................................................

**Exercise:** In this mindful focusing exercise, you don't start by looking at your thoughts. Instead you begin with your breath, noticing the feeling of the cool air washing over the back of your throat and into your lungs. You notice the feeling of your ribs expanding and contracting, and your diaphragm tensing and releasing as you let go of a breath. Keep observing your breathing and noticing each part of the physical experience.

As you focus on anything, your breath included, you'll always have thoughts. Take this opportunity, as you notice the experience of your breath, to be aware of what your mind is doing. As each thought comes up, observe it—*There's a thought*—and return your attention to your breath. So the sequence is breathe, acknowledge thought, and then return to the awareness of breathing.

Watching how thoughts intrude into your consciousness, even while you are focusing on something else, is a good way to recognize the power of the mind. No matter how you try to stay with the breath, thoughts keep showing up. This is normal and inevitable, but you are learning how to acknowledge your mind while staying with your physical experience.

Practice mindful focusing for five minutes or so. Repeat the exercise several times. Then ask yourself this question: How does mindful focusing change your relationship to your thoughts? Is there any shift in terms of their frequency, intensity, believability, or intrusiveness?

..............................................................................................

# 18

# Label and Let Go

## What You Need to Know

After you've learned to watch your thoughts, it's time to label them. Describing what your mind is doing creates distance from your thoughts, reducing how believable or compelling they seem.

One way to label thoughts is to use the phrase *I'm having the thought that* _____ : *I'm having the thought that I'm selfish. I'm having the thought that I will never get a promotion. I'm having a thought that the pain in my stomach is a tumor.* Notice how the mere act of labeling puts you further away from the cognition, often making it feel less urgent and authentic.

Another labeling technique uses the phrase *Now my mind is having a* _____ *thought.* The labels you can use for this exercise might include the following: fear thoughts, judgment thoughts, not-good-enough thoughts, mistake thoughts, should thoughts, and so on. Make up your own labels for categories of thinking you use often.

While you observe a sequence of cognitions, thought labeling might go like this: *Now my mind is having a self-critical thought... Now my mind is having a fear of the future thought... Now my mind is having an angry thought... Now my mind is having another fear of the future thought...* and so on.

# Taking It Further

The next stage in defusion involves letting go of each thought. Here are some easy exercises that will help you learn to let go.

.................................................................................

**Leaves on a stream:** Imagine each thought as an autumn leaf detaching from a tree and falling into a swiftly moving stream. As the leaf hits the water, it's caught in a current and is swept rapidly downstream, around a bend, and out of sight. Each new thought, as it shows up in your mind, is visualized as a newly fallen leaf, swept downstream and out of sight.

.................................................................................

**Billboards:** Imagine yourself driving down a long stretch of highway, with occasional billboards showing up on either side of the road. You can visualize each thought as a message on one of the billboards. Notice it briefly, then imagine your car sweeping past. As your thought goes out of sight, the next new thought is assigned to another billboard and is briefly noted until your car roars by.

.................................................................................

**Balloons:** Imagine a clown holding the strings to a dozen red balloons. As each new thought arrives, let a balloon detach from the group and watch it float up into the sky and out of sight. If the image moves too slowly and it takes too long for the balloons to drift out of sight, imagine a stiff wind blowing the balloons away.

.................................................................................

**Computer pop-ups:** Imagine each thought as a pop-up advertisement or reminder on your computer screen. Briefly note the thought, then let it disappear until the next pop-up shows up on the screen.

**Trains and boats:** You can imagine yourself at a railroad crossing, watching a slow freight train pass in front of you. Each boxcar becomes a new thought, rolling slowly by. Or you can imagine yourself on a bridge, watching fishing boats pass slowly beneath you on their way out to sea. Each boat can represent a thought, moving slowly out of sight.

**Physical letting go:** As each thought enters your mind, imagine that you are holding it in your hand, palm up. Slowly rotate your hand until your palm is facing down and imagine the thought dropping out of sight. Then return your hand to the palm-up position. As a new thought arrives, again turn your hand in a dropping motion. Physicalizing the letting-go process and allowing movement to symbolize the dropping of the thought can make the letting-go experience feel more powerful and real.

More in **Practice and Examples** at http://9813.nhpubs.com.

# 19

## Use Distancing Techniques

## What You Need to Know

There are defusion exercises that can help you distance from thoughts and take them less seriously. When you detach from thoughts, they have less power to make you sad or mad or scared. Distancing exercises have one thing in common: they embrace a painful thought while letting it shrink and diminish in importance. You'll understand that paradox as you explore the following distancing experiences.

.....................................................................................

**Exercise:** Your mind is trying to protect you. It's attempting to predict dangerous possibilities, trying to judge what's good or bad for you, and trying to figure out why things happen. So your mind is working hard to help you survive and overcome problems. As you know, however, your mind can run amok. It can obsessively focus on thoughts that do nothing but make you miserable. One way to deal with these thoughts is to thank your mind for its efforts to protect you. As each negative thought shows up, simply say, *Thank you, Mind, for that thought.*

You don't have to get involved with the thought; you don't have to understand or explore it. You can just appreciate that your mind gave you that thought in an effort to protect you. *Thank you, Mind* is a mantra that acknowledges your mind's goodwill while distancing you from the painful thoughts it throws at you: *Thank you, Mind, for that scary thought... Thank you, Mind, for that* I'm-no-good *thought... Thank you, Mind, for predicting failure... Thank you, Mind, for the thought that my relationship will collapse.*

While you keep thanking your mind, you're also distancing from each thought as it arises. You are appreciating your mind's efforts while recognizing that it may have gone astray.

# Taking It Further

Defusion is not about arguing with or disputing your thoughts. In practicing defusion, you seek to accept your thoughts in whatever form they take. Whether your thoughts are positive or negative, accurate or distorted, defusion encourages you to let your thoughts be what they are.

Sometimes, though, your mind will resist the defusion process. It will insist that a particular thought is important and that there will be dire consequences if you ignore it. This is just another thought, one in a long string, and no more true or important than any other. If a thought tenaciously returns again and again after you use the observing, labeling, and letting-go tools described in the previous sections, use the distancing drill below to explore its history, function, and workability. When it's clear that the thought hasn't helped you, just let it go.

**Exercise:** For thoughts that are particularly sticky and painful, or that show up frequently, we suggest you use the following four-step distancing drill whenever that thought shows up.

**Step 1. Ask yourself how old the thought is.** Did it start when you lost your job three years ago, does it go back to when your first wife asked for a divorce, do you remember having the thought in childhood? If you're not sure when it started, make a rough guess of how long it's been around—five years, ten, twenty?

**Step 2. Examine the function of the thought.** What is this thought in the service of? What behavior does the thought drive you to do or not do? Most negative thoughts have a single function. They're trying to help you prevent pain by avoiding a particular action or situation. So just ask yourself, *What is this thought trying to protect me from feeling and discourage me from doing?*

**Step 3. Examine the workability of the thought.** Is it helping you avoid pain, or is it just paralyzing you and making it hard to do the things that matter? For example, if you realize that a thought is trying to protect you from fear, you might examine whether you've been more or less fearful when you listen to that thought. And you might ask whether the thought is helping you do the things you want to do—or getting in your way. In the end, the answer to workability is a pretty simple yes or no. Either the thought is helping or it isn't.

**Step 4. Ask yourself whether you'd be willing to have this thought while still doing the things it's trying to scare you away from.** For example, if the thought is telling you to ignore an attractive person at a party because he or she might reject you, would you be willing to have the thought and talk to the person anyway? The question is this: Are you going to let your scary and discouraging thoughts control your behavior? Or are you going to let your mind say whatever it wants while you do the things that really matter in your life?

Whenever you use the distancing drill, you'll find that even the most painful and persistent thoughts seem less important and exert less influence. Instead of letting your mind discourage you from doing the things you care about, you can use defusion to get some distance from these paralyzing thoughts.

More in **Practice and Examples** at http://9813.nhpubs.com.

# 20

## Discover Secondary Emotions

## What You Need to Know

Your ultimate goal with anxiety isn't to eliminate it, but to moderate it and regulate it. The reality, as we have discussed in previous sections, is that you probably aren't going to be very successful in your attempts to get rid of anxiety anyway, and you wouldn't want to if you could. You need those anxious feelings in certain contexts. They quite literally keep you alive. When you step off a curb in front of an oncoming bus, you count on your fight-or-flight instincts to help you jump out of the way; and in the unlikely event that you actually *do* meet a mountain lion while out on a long hike alone, you'll want your anxious feelings then too. In short, you need to learn to better regulate your emotions so that you aren't perpetually trapped in an anxious loop, and you need to learn how to tolerate distress more effectively when it does arise.

In this section and the next four, we will cover five simple techniques that will help you learn to tolerate distress more effectively when it does arrive. In this section, you'll learn to distinguish primary from secondary emotions. Think about it this way: Some of us spend a long time not even realizing that what we are experiencing is anxiety. Even more of us can't distinguish between the initial anxious feelings we experience and the emotions these feelings bring up in turn. As a result, we get buried in anxiety before we know it, and the tidal wave of feelings accompanying our anxiety sucks us down into a vortex of pain.

**Exercise:** The first step to better regulating your anxiety is to catch this process while it is happening. As you move through your day today and for the next two days, slow down long enough to notice your anxious feelings as they arise and then notice the emotions these anxious feelings bring up after they have arisen. Doing this will help you step back and get a better·picture of how anxiety works in your life. From this position, you may be able to make better, healthier decisions about how you react to your anxious feelings. That doesn't necessarily mean the anxiety itself will dissipate (at least not at first), but it does hold the promise of helping you behave in a way aligned with your values instead of simply reacting to anxiety.

## Taking It Further

Emotions are nuanced, multidimensional responses to thoughts or situations. Our initial emotional response is often referred to as our *primary emotion.* This is the feeling that immediately comes up in a particular circumstance. For example, if you won the lottery tomorrow, your primary emotion would probably be excitement. In addition to our primary emotions, we also have *secondary emotions,* or feelings about our feelings (Marra 2005). The excitement that winning the lottery initially caused you may bring up other feelings—you may feel surprised about how excited you actually became about winning the lottery, for example.

It's easy to see how, with more complex emotional material than winning a lottery, your secondary emotions could quickly escalate into a chain of very positive or very painful feelings depending on the context. Here is a slightly more complex example: Imagine that you have to give a presentation at work tomorrow in front of thirty colleagues you respect tremendously. You're terrified of public speaking, so you've been putting off dealing with the presentation, and now you feel underprepared. You haven't really done your research. Panic creeps in because you're certain you'll make a complete fool of yourself. You get angry at yourself and begin berating yourself for your poor time management. Later, still anxious about the talk, you allow yourself to sink down into a spiral of shame and avoidance. You sit on the sofa eating ice cream in front of the TV instead of doing the work you know you should be doing. More anxiety comes up, then anger, and more shame, and on and on it goes until you finally have a terrible panic attack.

Here's the thing with a situation like this: The initial anxiety, as uncomfortable as it is, really isn't as bad as the chain of emotions it later sets off. If you have a phobia of public speaking, it's improbable that you'll simply be able to shut down the anxiety that giving a presentation at work may bring up. However, most of the chain of emotional pain that happens in the example above is unnecessary. These secondary emotions would have never come up if, at any point, you had made some intervention. Even better, had you simply faced and accepted the initial anxiety in the first place, none of the secondary emotions would have come into play at all.

This is why recognizing your emotions and differentiating between primary and secondary emotions is an integral part of emotional regulation. You aren't going to be able to eliminate all of the painful emotions in your life, but you can regulate your emotional experience by better understanding it and then making some choices about how to behave in a given situation.

**Exercise:** Think back to a recent situation that caused you extreme anxiety. Bring it to mind and visualize it in as much detail as you can muster. Then see if you can tease apart the primary emotions from the secondary emotions. How could you have changed your emotional experience by intervening earlier in the cycle of emotion? (Here's a hint: any of the techniques in this book may help.) What could you do next time anxiety arises in your life? Make a commitment to yourself to try this the next time you begin to feel anxious. See what happens.

# 21

# Work on Anxiety-Making Behavior Patterns

## What You Need to Know

People who are anxious often, without even realizing it, develop behaviors that only serve to create more anxiety or reinforce existing anxiety. On the surface this statement may sound preposterous. Why would an anxious person possibly do something to make herself more anxious?

One answer is embedded in the example about public speaking in the previous section. When we feel anxious, we seek out ways to diminish our anxiety. We look for a quick fix for our anxious feelings, and sometimes those fixes even seem to work in the short term. Avoidance is a classic example. When you put off preparing for a presentation at work because you are anxious about public speaking, you are engaging in avoidance. If you dread flying and you always choose to drive, this too is avoidance. If you're worried your lover is going to send you a nasty email because of the fight you had last night and you choose not to check your email, guess what? That's avoidance too.

Of course, avoidance isn't the only behavior pattern that is anxiety provoking. Checking is another example. Perhaps you're worried about that email from your lover and instead of avoiding it, you click over to your mailbox every two minutes in the hopes she won't send the nasty communiqué after all. Or you can't seem to shake the fear that you left the coffee pot on, so you go back into the house to check several times, just to make sure. Both of these are checking behaviors.

........................................................................................

**Exercise:** For the next week, keep an anxiety journal. Every time you have an anxious feeling, write down what you did during and after the feeling arose. At the end of the week, review your list and assess whether or not there are any patterns or relationships between how you behave and how you feel. In the next exercise, you'll use this journal as a jumping-off point.

........................................................................................

# Taking It Further

The tricky, even seductive, thing about anxiety-driven behaviors is that they can actually reduce your anxiety in the short term. If you're afraid of flying and you don't fly, you won't feel anxious. Going back in the house to make sure the coffee pot is off—even doing it a couple of times—seems rational. After all, you don't want the house to burn down, and it does reduce your anxiety. So why not avoid or check or engage in any of the other behaviors you've developed to reduce your anxiety in the short term?

Because in the long run these behaviors typically only serve to reinforce patterns that will eventually lead to more anxiety, and they lead to a whole array of nasty downstream psychological effects you're probably better off not dealing with. You're going to have to give that presentation at work. We've already illustrated what's going to happen if you avoid the anxiety by putting off the speech. So why not just engage it? The email will either come from your lover or it won't. No amount of checking or avoiding is going to change the outcome.

Perhaps worse, these behaviors have the power to make your life smaller. Sure, you could avoid the anxiety that flying causes by never taking another plane trip. But what do you sacrifice by making that choice? Are you willing to never cross the Atlantic because you fear flying? And what if you're anxious about a job interview or a relationship? Should you go jobless or be alone to serve your anxiety?

Like so many things in life, altering anxiety-driven behaviors isn't a black-and-white issue. In some cases avoidance is good. Only a fool would put himself in a tiger cage to overcome his fear of being eaten by a giant cat. Leaving on a coffee pot isn't likely to burn down the house, but burning embers in the fireplace may indeed—better to check in that case and see whether or not your home is in danger.

The whole point of emotional regulation strategies is not to develop a black-and-white sensibility about "healthy" and "unhealthy" psychological responses. Instead, it's about moderation and regulation. You could look at and work on some of the behavioral patterns that cause anxiety in your life and provide yourself more room to move by doing so.

...................................................................................

**Exercise:** Review the notes you kept for the previous exercise and think about what you might do differently to break this cycle. For example, if you are engaged in avoidance or checking, you could choose to take some deep breaths and then behave differently. Map out what you might do differently with a recurring checking or avoid-ance behavior next time, and use the mindfulness and relaxation techniques outlined earlier in this book to help guide you through these times. Watch what happens to your anxiety over time as you behave differently. In the Practice and Examples segment, you'll find a chart you can use to track what happens when you try different behaviors.

...............................................................................................

More in **Practice and Examples** at http://9813.nhpubs.com.

# 22

# Identify Trigger Thoughts

## What You Need to Know

In truth, there are some things to be anxious about in life. Distress, in many different forms, is a fundamental part of the human experience. The only people who never feel distress are comatose or dead—states of being you hopefully aren't aspiring to at this moment. As the Buddha once said, "Life is suffering." It is many other things as well, but this truth is one most of us try too often to ignore.

The key to coping with anxiety more successfully is not to eliminate it, but to temper it; to tease apart the difference between the immediate experience of anxiety and its downstream psychological effects; and to allow yourself the opportunity to experience a broader array of emotions instead of simply getting trapped in your stressful and anxious feelings. In this section, you'll delve into your personal anxiety trigger thoughts. These are called *trigger thoughts* (McKay, Rogers, and McKay 2003) because they trigger our anxiety. The thoughts in the bullet list that follows are all examples of trigger thoughts. Let's start with an example: *There's good evidence that if human beings don't change their relationship to the environment, global warming could set off a series of catastrophic events that would alter our planet forever.*

Does that thought make you feel anxious? It makes us feel anxious too. Here are a few more thoughts that may make you feel anxious:

- *I'm going to fail at...*

- *I can't handle* _____ , *and I'm going to get anxious.*

- *My life is filled with so many responsibilities; I can't handle it all.*

- *If I get on that plane tomorrow, it could explode.*

- *What if* _____ *happened? I couldn't stand it.*

..............................................................................................

**Exercise:** For one week, each time you start to get anxious, try to pin down the anxiety trigger thought that is at the root of the feeling. Keep a journal of these anxious thoughts. Do the same thoughts occur again and again? Look for any patterns or trigger thoughts that are consistently associated with your anxiety. Just identifying them may help you regulate the emotional experience you have with them. Or you can take it a step further and sit mindfully and watch the thought, expose it to some reality testing, or try any of the other techniques in the book. Do what works for you.

..............................................................................................

# Taking It Further

Clearly there is a relationship between what we think and how we feel. Some thoughts make just about everyone anxious. Anyone who takes climate change seriously is bound to be concerned by it. Other thoughts are specific to individuals and trigger an anxiety response in them yet may not trigger the same response in someone else.

Since our brains are such wonderful thought-creation devices, trigger thoughts can be tricky to track down. You may not even know what the underlying trigger thought is that drives your anxiety, and even if you do, you may not hear it every time it comes up. To better cope with distress and regulate your emotions, one excellent technique is to identify your trigger thoughts. In the next exercise, you'll expand upon the list you started in the previous exercise.

..................................................................................

**Exercise:** For a week, jot down each time you feel anxious. But this time, instead of writing down just the trigger thought, also write down the associated behavior. As you become more skilled at identifying your trigger thoughts and the behaviors you engage in in reaction to them, there is a broad array of techniques you can use to challenge the thoughts, mitigate the pain they cause, or change the behaviors that result from them. In the online segment of this section, you'll find an Emotional Record chart you can use to further understand the connections between the things that happen in your life, the way you think and feel, and how you subsequently behave.

..................................................................................

More in **Practice and Examples** at http://9813.nhpubs.com.

# 23

## Make Room for Positive Feelings

## What You Need to Know

Do you take time for yourself and do something you enjoy regularly? Do you give yourself the opportunity for positive emotions like joy, happiness, peace, and serenity to arise? Or are you like most of us, constantly rushing from place to place, buried in responsibilities, always looking forward toward the next thing that "has to" or "should be" done instead of being where you are in the present? If so, this is a sure way to create more anxiety and strife in your life.

Think about it this way: We *are* what we *do*. Monks who sit on the mountain in quiet solitude aren't peaceful and serene and connected to nature by some weird accident. They have that experience because their environment, their society, and their lifestyle facilitate it. Take that same person and place him in the madness of modern life, and he is almost certain to change.

If you wake up in the morning thirty minutes before work, slurp down three cups of coffee, skip breakfast, rush the kids to day care, sit in traffic cursing because you're late, get into the office twenty minutes late, rush to your first meeting of the day, fumble through that, then go back to your desk and madly try to sort through email until lunch only to find the day running away from you as you wonder who will pick up the kids tonight and what you're going to prepare for dinner, and you don't ever offer yourself a break or do something you enjoy, guess what? You're probably going to get anxious. Who wouldn't? A hundred bucks says that if you traded places with that monk for just a few days you'd feel a lot more peaceful and he'd feel a lot more anxious.

.................................................................................

**Exercise:** Anxious people tend to get caught in anxiety-making behavioral patterns. Take a look at your life. Do you even provide yourself the possibility of peace? For the next several days, jot down a rough outline of your daily schedule. Do you make any time for pleasure? Can you pinpoint any habits or mindless patterns that contribute to making your days feel overscheduled and stressful?
.................................................................................

# Taking It Further

If you want to minimize distress in your life, you must take the time to do something you like every day. It doesn't have to be big—just doing a few small things you enjoy could make the difference between an anxious day and a joyous one. Below are a few examples of things you could do, but we'd bet you have a better idea of what you enjoy than we do. So just think about what you like and allow yourself to do it. And if you think you don't have time to enjoy your life, you may want to reconsider that policy— your life depends on it.

- Go for a hike in the woods.

- Chat on the phone with a friend.

- Do some deep breathing

- Listen to music you enjoy.

- Invite a friend to lunch at your favorite restaurant.

- Read a fun book.

- Do some gardening.

- Try out yoga.

- Get down on the floor and play with your kids—and put thoughts of chores you "should" be doing aside.

- Enjoy a piece of dark chocolate.

- Watch some comedy on TV or the computer.

More in **Practice and Examples** at http://9813.nhpubs.com.

# 24

# Use Distraction and Self-Soothing

## What You Need to Know

When you're in the midst of a panic attack or when you're dealing with some very serious anxiety, you may not have the bandwidth to assess your thoughts and behaviors or think through activities that bring you joy. In fact, just getting through the day can be tough if you're truly overwhelmed with anxious feelings. In this case some "emergency" interventions may be in order. Such interventions are part of tolerating distress and better regulating your emotions as well, and in the remainder of this part of the book we want to focus on two of the more useful emergency interventions: distraction and self-soothing. You'll find these techniques actually fit hand in glove with what has come previously in this part of the book.

......................................................................................

**Exercise:** Before using distraction and self-soothing, it's important to get into a mental space where you understand how these techniques differ from avoidance and some of the other anxiety-making behaviors we discussed previously. In avoidance, for example, you take a stance where you choose not to deal with a distressing situation. But when you apply distraction and self-soothing in moments when you feel overwhelmed by anxiety, it's with the knowledge that you intend to deal with the situation in the future, and you're only using the techniques to calm your emotions to the point that you can think and act effectively. Before moving ahead, think of any recent situations where distraction and self-soothing might have helped you get into a calmer, problem-solving state of mind. What does a state of emotional emergency feel like for you? Get prepared to recognize it if it happens again, so you will be ready to to take action by engaging in distracting or self-soothing activities and sensations.

...........................................................................

# Taking It Further

These techniques can also help you treat yourself more compassionately—the way you might treat a friend who was really freaking out. Give yourself a break. Think about all of the pain you've suffered in life, all of the stress you labor under. Does it really make sense to live life this way? Couldn't you give yourself a break and allow some space to feel peaceful and relaxed?

We hope the answer is a vehement yes! If so, try any of the following to distract yourself or soothe yourself when those anxious feelings start to arise. Later, when you've cooled off, you can come back and try the other exercises in this book to help manage your long-term experience with anxiety.

- Sit in a dark, quiet room, light some candles, and burn some incense.

- Try calming visualizations, such as thinking of an ocean or a forest.

- Get a massage. Trade massages with your partner or friend if you can't get one from a professional.

- Exercise.

- Take a meandering walk through an interesting neighborhood.

- Go to a sauna at your local health club.

- Take a long, hot bath with scented salts or oils.

- Chat online with a friend.

- Visit your favorite websites.

- Give someone a hug or ask someone to give you a hug.

- Pick some flowers and put them in a vase in your office or home.

These small gestures, along with everything else in this section, ultimately come down to a simple practice: nourishing yourself. Do that and your anxiety will diminish naturally.

We hear a lot about "the middle path"—that third way that is neither black nor white, up nor down, but staunchly in between. Emotional regulation is a kind of middle path. It's not about turning off anxiety; it's about moderating it. To better tolerate distress, you don't need to punish yourself, and you don't need to be pathological about exposing yourself to what stresses you out. You don't need to be fascist in your attempts to regulate your emotions. You can move toward a life of less stress and greater joy gently. In fact, gently is the *only* way you will get there. Be compassionate with yourself—compassionately encourage yourself to face your fear, compassionately move toward instead of away from distress, and when you need a break, compassionately give it to yourself. When you do this, when you care for yourself, compassion will slowly seep into your life as anxiety leaks away.

More in **Practice and Examples** at http://9813.nhpubs.com.

# Part 4

# Basic Wellness

You haven't moved off the couch in weeks, got only three hours of sleep last night, and had half a bag of corn chips and a diet soda for breakfast this morning...and to top it off, you're supposed to give a major presentation at the office today. Do you think your exercise, diet, and sleep habits are going to ease or aggravate your anxiety about this career-making-or-breaking event? There are hard questions in *Thirty-Minute Therapy for Anxiety*. This is not one of them.

You are a complicated piece of biology. That brain of yours that keeps spinning out anxious thoughts is connected to the rest of you. Taking good care of yourself may not eliminate your anxiety, but it can do you a whole lot of good—and leave you better prepared to help yourself live well with anxious thoughts. There are also specific lifestyle factors that do have a demonstrated connection to anxiety.

In part 4, you'll learn some basics about getting the rest and sleep you need, eating well, and moving your body as part of your general plan for living well with anxiety.

# 25 Sleep Hygiene

## What You Need to Know

If you've ever had a sleepless night, you know what life can be like the next morning—when you drop your coffee cup in the toilet, send the kids off to school with dog food sandwiches, and try to feed your puzzled pet a bowl of peanut butter and jelly. To feel and perform your best, you need to get restful, high-quality sleep most of the time.

If you have a long history of poor sleep or the symptoms of any recognized sleep disorder, consult with a doctor or another health care provider. There may be underlying causes that need treatment. If you have only recently developed problems with sleeping or infrequently have trouble sleeping, here's where to start:

- **Cut down on caffeine, or avoid it entirely.** Caffeine affects people differently. If you're very sensitive to its effects, a single cup of coffee in the morning may interfere with your sleep that night (Landolt et al. 1995). If you're finding it hard to sleep, try to limit your consumption of caffeinated beverages to the morning hours. If you're sensitive to caffeine or are having persistent trouble falling asleep, try phasing out caffeine entirely.

- **Get enough exercise.** Experts are divided on whether vigorous exercise in the hours just before bed makes it harder to sleep, and the answer may vary from person to person. But no one disputes that regular strenuous exercise at some point in the day has a beneficial effect on sleep (and just about every other area of life). It's common sense that you'll have an easier time falling asleep if your body has been taxed physically during the day. See section 28 for more on exercise.

## Taking It Further

Once you've adjusted your caffeine intake and considered whether your exercise routine (or lack thereof) is playing havoc with your sleep, it's time to master the basics of sleep hygiene:

- Select a mattress, pillows, and bedding that you find comfortable. Trial and error are necessary here. There is no magic mattress that will meet everyone's sleep needs.

- Go to bed at the same time each evening.

- Keep your bedroom as dark as possible and make sure it's a comfortable temperature—not too hot or too cold.

- Reserve your bedroom for sleeping and making love. Don't use it as an office, a television room, or a library.

# 26 Insomnia and Solutions

## What You Need to Know

About 30 percent of American adults suffer from insomnia. Among the more common lifestyle conditions, insomnia has perhaps the most potential to make feelings of anxiety worse. Although this varies greatly, most of us need between seven to eight hours of sleep per night and won't feel well rested if we get less than six hours of uninterrupted sleep. The deep sleep that replenishes and repairs the tissues in your body occurs early during your sleep period, while rapid eye movement, or REM sleep—the kind of sleep during which you tend to dream—happens later in the cycle. REM sleep appears to be necessary for cognitive function and mental clarity. If these sleep cycles are interrupted, systems throughout your body can suffer.

In addition to the problems mentioned in section 25, here are some other issues you might want to consider:

- **Anxiety about sleep.** Since you're reading about anxiety, it seems a little ridiculous for us to warn you about the further dangers of worrying about not getting enough sleep. But this phenomenon can be a big deal and something of a vicious cycle: you start not getting enough sleep, and this makes your anxiety worse, so you worry more about not getting enough sleep, and so on. The work you do here will help improve your situation generally, but you should also consider moving on to something other than just lying there if you find you're unable to fall asleep after thirty minutes or so in bed. Get up and go read a book, finish up the night's dishes, or do some other quiet activity. After a period of time, you can try to fall asleep again.

- **Emotional or physical stimulation in the evening.** Anything that gets you wound up in the later evening can interfere with your sleep that night. Depending on your disposition, you might be able to watch thrillers or have an argument with your cousin Freddy on the phone, or you might not. If you find yourself feeling overly excited by your evening's activity, make a point of switching to calming activities— like reading (especially nonfiction), bathing, playing solitaire, or meditating—for a couple of hours before bed.

- **Light.** Recent studies suggest that exposure to certain colors of light can result in sleep disruption (Revell and Skene 2007). Blue light, in particular, seems to be the worst offender, and computer screens are notorious emitters of blue light. If you engage in any screen time after dark, you may want to consider installing a free application on your computer called f.lux (http://stereopsis.com/flux/). This little application makes a note of your location on the planet and, when it gets dark in your area, resets the light output of your screen to dramatically reduce the higher-temperature blue light. The result is a pleasantly rose-colored screen display that may reduce the alertness-inducing effects of blue light.

- **Routine.** We often talk about "catching up" on missed sleep, but feeling well-rested depends more on a regular routine of good sleep than it does on occasional rounds of hibernating until noon. The body has a sleep-wakefulness cycle, called the *circadian cycle*, which it goes through every day—ideally about sixteen to seventeen hours out of bed and seven to eight in bed. This cycle will function much more smoothly, ensuring better sleep, if you retire and get up at the same times every day, so doing so should be your goal. Many people have difficulty sleeping Sunday night, having stayed up late on the two weekend nights and sleeping in too late the next mornings. It's very common for people who suffer from insomnia to go to bed and get up at irregular times. The extreme case of sleep disruption is working different shifts back to back. Unless you must, it's best to avoid jobs that require you to continually change your shift. Over time, you will lose a lot of sleep and may compromise your health.

- **Uncomfortable sleeping environment.** Your sleep environment may be subtly undermining your sleep. A mattress that is either too soft or too firm is a common problem. If at all possible, invest in a quality mattress that feels truly comfortable to you. The same applies for pillows (you want something more comfortable than what you'd find in the average motel). As mentioned, room temperature is also an important variable; many people have problems sleeping if the room temperature is over 80 degrees. If you don't have air conditioning, use a fan to cool your room. The optimal temperature for sleep is about 70 degrees. Noise and light can also be problems. If you can't escape noise, get a fan or white noise machine to help mask it. If there's excess light, dark curtains or eye shades will often help.

- **Noisy partners.** If you have one, your bed partner is a critical part of your sleep environment. Loud snoring is a very common disrupter of sleep that affects millions of people who simply lie there and put up with it. There are many snoring solutions (including sprays and nose guards that you can get at your local drugstore as well as hundreds of devices you'll find on the Internet). Or you may want to go to an otolaryngologist who specializes in the treatment of snoring. For more severe cases, laser surgery or surgical techniques using high-frequency radio waves have been used effectively. Snoring is not something you have to live with.

# Taking It Further

Also keep these don'ts in mind:

- **Don't have a heavy meal before bedtime—but don't go to bed hungry either.** A small, healthy snack just before bedtime can be helpful.

- **Don't indulge in heavy alcohol consumption before bedtime.** For some people, a small glass of wine before bed may help, but your alcohol consumption should not exceed this.

- **Don't use tobacco.** Nicotine is a mild stimulant, and apart from its more publicized health risks, it can interfere with sleep. If you are a smoker, talk to your doctor about the best ways to curtail this habit.

- **Don't engage in nonsleep activities in bed.** Unless they are part of your sleep ritual, avoid activities such as working or reading in bed. This will help strengthen the association between bed and sleep.

- **Don't use pillows that are too high or too puffy.** Feather pillows, which compress, are best.

- **Don't nap during the day.** Short catnaps of fifteen to twenty minutes are okay, but long naps of an hour or more may interfere with your sleep the following night.

- **Don't let yourself be afraid of insomnia.** Work on accepting those nights when you don't sleep well. You can still function the next day, even if you've had only a couple of hours of sleep. The less you fight, resist, or fear sleeplessness, the more it will tend to go away.

More in **Practice and Examples** at http://9813.nhpubs.com.

# 27     Diet

## What You Need to Know

If there is one thing people are anxious about in this world (or at least in the United States), it's whether they're eating a healthful diet—or, at least, whether they're eating the diet most healthful for them. If you fall into this group, you can experiment with a few simple strategies.

As we said in section 25, it's pretty widely accepted that caffeine can interfere with sleep and can also aggravate anxiety. Our first suggestions for you if you're struggling with anxiety is to decrease or eliminate your intake of coffee, tea, cola, other caffeinated beverages, and chocolate.

Although it may be a difficult fact to face if you have a sweet tooth, sugar is another big culprit in emotional dysregulation. Ups and downs in blood sugar frequently contribute to anxiety and a self-perpetuating cycle of hyper high followed by rock-bottom crash. And what happens after that? You crave more sugar, and the cycle starts again.

.......................................................................................

**Exercise:** Keep a food diary for a week—but not just any food diary. If you've ever tried to lose weight, chances that you've already tried keeping track of what you consume. Give it a try again, but this time, add descriptions of how you feel at and between meals. See if you can chart the effects of caffeine, sugar, protein, and fat consumption on your anxiety. Are there certain meal patterns or foods that keep you on an even keel? How is your mood affected by overeating, skipping meals, or eating while distracted or under extreme stress?

# Taking It Further

If you struggle with weight, have type 2 diabetes, suffer from food allergies or gastrointestinal problems, or wrestle with any other food-related problems, finding a diet that promotes your health without leaving you feeling famished and deprived is obviously an important step in lessening your feelings of anxiety related to these issues. Specific advice about eating well for any of these conditions is beyond the scope of this book, but if you're having health problems, you may find it useful to apply the problem-solving techniques you'll find in sections 13 and 14 to your attempts at dietary behavior change.

# 28  Exercise

## What You Need to Know

One of the most effective ways to reduce anxiety is also one of the simplest: regular, vigorous aerobic exercise. How does exercise reduce anxiety? Regular, sustained physical activity has a positive effect on some of the body systems that are related to anxiety. For example, exercise reduces muscle tension, helps your body process excess adrenaline and thyroxin more rapidly, releases frustration, increases oxygen to the blood and brain, stimulates endorphins (the body's natural feel-good chemicals), improves digestion and circulation, lowers blood pressure, and improves elimination.

If you haven't been exercising, it's important not to start too quickly or intensely. Doing so often results in prematurely burning out on the idea of maintaining a regular exercise program.

## Taking It Further

The following guidelines for getting started are recommended:

- **Approach exercise gradually.** Set limited goals at the outset, such as exerting yourself for only ten minutes (or to the point of being winded) every other day for the first week. Add five minutes to your workout time each successive week until you reach thirty minutes.

- **Commit to a trial period.** Make a commitment to stay with your program for one month, despite aches and pains, inertia, or other resistance to exercise. By the end of the first month, you may start to experience sufficient benefits to make the exercise self-motivating. Be aware that it can take three to four months or more to achieve a high level of fitness after being out of shape.

- **Keep track of your exercise.** Use the Daily Record of Exercise in the online Practice and Examples material to keep track of the date, time, duration, and type of exercise you engage in on a daily basis. If you're doing aerobic exercise, record your pulse immediately after completing your workout and enter it under the column labeled "Pulse Rate." Also be sure to rate your level of satisfaction, using a 0 to 10 scale, where 0 equals no satisfaction at all and 10 equals total satisfaction with your exercise experience. As you begin to get into shape, your satisfaction should increase. Finally, if you fail to exercise when you intended to, indicate your reason for not doing so. Later on it may be useful to reevaluate these reasons to see if they are truly valid and address them if so. For example, you might move your exercise time to later in the day if you find you just don't have the time in the morning. (See the online portion of this section for ways to deal with resistance to exercise.)

- **Warm up.** Your body needs a gradual warm-up before engaging in vigorous exercise. This is especially important if you are over age forty. Five minutes of calisthenics or stretching exercises will usually be sufficient.

- **Expect minor discomfort.** Aches and pains are normal when you're starting out, especially if you've gotten out of shape. You can expect the discomfort to pass as you improve your strength and endurance.

- **Try to focus on the process of exercise rather than the product.** Pay attention to the inherently enjoyable aspects of the exercise itself. If you like to run or ride your bike, it helps to have a scenic environment. Keep in mind that focusing on competition with others or yourself tends to increase rather than reduce anxiety and stress.

- **Reward yourself for maintaining a commitment to your exercise program.** Give yourself dinner out, a weekend trip, or new athletic clothes or equipment in exchange for sticking to your program during the first weeks and months.

- **Cool down.** After vigorous exercise, it is important to give yourself a few minutes to cool down. Walking around for two or three minutes will help bring blood back from peripheral muscles to the rest of your body.

- **Avoid exercising within ninety minutes of a meal, and don't eat until one hour after exercising.**

- **Avoid exercising when you feel ill or overstressed.** Try a deep relaxation technique instead.

- **Stop exercising if you experience any sudden, unexplainable bodily symptoms.**

- **Keep exercise interesting.** If you find yourself feeling bored with exercising solo, find a partner to go with you or a form of exercise that requires a partner.

- **Try to exercise more than once a week.** Engaging in infrequent spurts of exercise is stressful to your body and generally does more harm than good (walking is an exception).

More in **Practice and Examples** at http://9813.nhpubs.com.

# Some Other Resources

We hope you've learned a lot of practical things you can do to loosen anxiety's grip on your life. Nevertheless, we also realize that this book can probably contain instructions for only the first few steps in your journey to a life unrestricted by anxiety, fear, worry, and panic. Depending on your situation, disposition, and goals, you might decide to supplement the material in this book with medical therapy or psychotherapy. Or you might decide that you want to learn more about the approaches in some of the sections in the book. The resources in this section will get you started in the right direction.

## General Information About Anxiety

Bourne, Edmund J. 2011. *The Anxiety and Phobia Workbook.* Oakland, CA: New Harbinger.

## Cognitive Behavioral Therapy

Davis, Martha, Fanning, Patrick, and McKay, Matthew. 2007. *Thoughts and Feelings.* Oakland, CA: New Harbinger Publications.

## Relaxation and Stress Reduction

Davis, Martha, McKay, Matthew, Fanning, Patrick, and Eshelman, Elizabeth. 2008. *The Relaxation and Stress Reduction Workbook.* Oakland, CA: New Harbinger Publications.

## Help Especially for Specific Phobias

Antony, Martin A., and Watling, Mark. 2006. *Overcoming Medical Phobias.* Oakland, CA: New Harbinger Publications.

Antony, Martin A., and McCabe, Randi. 2005. *Overcoming Animal and Insect Phobias.* Oakland, CA: New Harbinger Publications.

Antony, Martin A., and Rowa, Karen. 2007. *Overcoming Fear of Heights.* Oakland, CA: New Harbinger Publications.

Antony, Martin A., and Owens, Katharine M. B. 2011. *Overcoming Health Anxiety.* Oakland, CA: New Harbinger Publications.

## Help Especially for Obsessive-Compulsive Disorder

Munford, Paul. 2004. *Overcoming Compulsive Hoarding.* Oakland, CA: New Harbinger Publications.

Munford, Paul. 2004. *Overcoming Compulsive Checking.* Oakland, CA: New Harbinger Publications.

Purdon, Christine, and Clark, David A. 2005. *Overcoming Obsessive Thoughts.* Oakland, CA: New Harbinger Publications.

Munford, Paul. 2005. *Overcoming Compulsive Washing.* Oakland, CA: New Harbinger Publications.

Hyman, Bruce, and DuFrene, Troy. 2008. *Coping with OCD.* Oakland, CA: New Harbinger Publications.

Hyman, Bruce, and Pedrick, Cherry. 2010. *The OCD Workbook.* Oakland, CA: New Harbinger Publications.

## Starting and Deepening a Mindfulness Practice

Brantley, Jeffrey, and Millstine, Wendy. 2007. *Calming Your Anxious Mind.* Oakland, CA: New Harbinger Publications.

## Acceptance and Commitment Therapy

Hayes, Steven C., and Smith, Spencer. 2005. *Get Out of Your Mind and Into Your Life.* Oakland, CA: New Harbinger Publications.

LeJeune, Chad. 2007. *The Worry Trap.* Oakland, CA: New Harbinger Publications.

Eifert, Georg H., and Forsyth, John P. 2008. *The Mindfulness and Acceptance Workbook for Anxiety.* Oakland, CA: New Harbinger Publications.

Wilson, Kelly G., and DuFrene, Troy. 2010. *Things Might Go Terribly, Horribly Wrong.* Oakland, CA: New Harbinger Publications.

## Dialectical Behavior Therapy

McKay, Matthew, Wood, Jeffrey C., and Brantley, Jeffrey. 2007. *The Dialectical Behavior Therapy Skills Workbook.* Oakland, CA: New Harbinger Publications.

Spradlin, Scott. 2003. *Don't Let Your Emotions Run Your Life.* Oakland, CA: New Harbinger Publications.

# References

American Psychiatric Association. 2000. *Diagnostic and Statistical Manual of Mental Disorders.* 4th ed., text revision. Washington, DC: Author.

Benson, H. 1975. *The Relaxation Response.* New York: Morrow.

Craske, M. G., and D. H. Barlow. 2008. "Panic Disorder and Agoraphobia." In *Clinical Handbook of Psychological Disorders: A Step-by-Step Treatment Manual,* edited by D. H. Barlow. New York: Guilford Press.

D'Zurilla, T. J., and M. R. Goldfried. 1971. "Problem Solving and Behavior Modification." *Journal of Abnormal Psychology* 78(1):107-126.

Hayes, S. C., K. D. Strosahl, and K. G. Wilson. 1999. *Acceptance and Commitment Therapy: An Experiential Approach to Behavior Change.* New York: Guilford Press.

Jacobson, E. 1929. *Progressive Relaxation.* Chicago: University of Chicago Press.

Kabat-Zinn, J. 1994. *Wherever You Go, There You Are: Mindfulness Meditation in Everyday Life.* New York: Hyperion.

Kessler, R. C., K. A. McGonagle, S. Zhao, C. B. Nelson, M. Hughes, S. Eshleman, et al. 1994. "Lifetime and 12-Month Prevalence of *DSM-III-R* Psychiatric Disorders in the United States. Results from the National Comorbidity Survey." *Archives of General Psychiatry* 51(1):8-19.

Landolt, H., E. Werth, A. Borbély, and D. Dijk, D. 1995. "Caffeine Intake (200 mg) in the Morning Affects Human Sleep and EEG Power Spectra at Night." *Brain Research* 675(1-2):67-74

Marra. 2005. *Dialectical Behavior Therapy in Private Practice.* Oakland, CA: New Harbinger.

Masi, N. 1993. *Breath of Life: Breathing Retraining.* Plantation, FL: Resource Warehouse.

McKay, M., P. Rogers, and J. McKay. 2003. *When Anger Hurts: Quieting the Storm Within.* 2nd ed. Oakland, CA: New Harbinger

Osborn, A. F. 1963. *Applied Imagination: Principles and Procedures of Creative Problem Solving.* 3rd ed. New York: Scribner.

Revell, V. L., and D. J. Skene. 2007. "Light-Induced Melatonin Suppression in Humans with Polychromatic and Monochromatic Light." *Chronobiology International* 24(6): 1125-1137.

Titchener, E. B. 1916. *A Text-Book of Psychology.* New York: Macmillan.

**Matthew McKay, PhD,** is a professor at the Wright Institute in Berkeley, CA. He has authored and coauthored numerous books, including *The Relaxation and Stress Reduction Workbook, Self-Esteem, Thoughts and Feelings,* and *Mind and Emotions.* In private practice, he specializes in the cognitive behavioral treatment of anxiety, anger, and depression.

**Troy DuFrene** is a writer who lives and works in the San Francisco Bay Area.

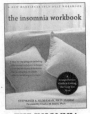

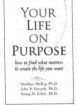